JAPAN

GOVERNMENT - POLITICS

JAPAN

Government—Politics

by

Robert Karl Reischauer
PRINCETON UNIVERSITY

THOMAS NELSON AND SONS
NEW YORK   **MCMXXXIX**

Copyright, 1939
Thomas Nelson and Sons

Printed in the United States of America
by the Haddon Craftsmen, Inc.

FOREWORD

DR. REISCHAUER did not live to complete this study. In his other published writings, in his lectures, in his notes, and in his conversations, he conveyed the unmistakable impression that he had no thought to predict the ultimate future of Japan. With a clear understanding, however, he saw what was to come in China; and with a clear logic he explained why it was inevitable, unless fate brought hurried relief that man seemed incapable of bringing. No man realized more keenly than he the conflicts inside Japan; the conflicts which he analyzed here, within this alien governmental apparatus thrust upon Japanese ideology and traditions; and the more fundamental conflicts deep within that very ideology and tradition, which the impact of modern occidental civilization has produced.

He could not know that he was early to be destroyed in the destructive outburst he foresaw. Could he have known, nothing would have grieved him more than the knowledge that in him Japan would lose a useful friend. He did not expect to solve the problems he was able to see; he did not expect to see them all. He had no desire to justify Japan, or anything Japanese, before the world.

If he could arouse a student's sympathetic interest in Japanese government and the political problems that face the people of Japan today, then he, who died while creating just such interest among American students on the very scene, would have found *his* justification for these pages.

PREFACE

It was my husband's conviction that in writing about Japanese government he could not take it for granted that the average American college student has that background of information which he brings to the study of the political institutions of almost any Western country. Consequently, he thought that his discussion of Japan's government must of necessity be much simpler and a great deal less scholarly than the sections in this series dealing with European and American politics. Indeed, he decided at the very outset that he would make no attempt to ferret out new facts. Because of his own interests in both Japanese political thought and in Japanese social history, however, and also because of his birth and some twenty years of residence in Japan, he felt, when requested to write about the Japanese government, justified in doing so because he believed he might be able to make a contribution, not to the facts, but to the interpretation of the facts relating to Japanese political institutions.

In the last section, which discusses the development of the Japanese government from the promulgation of the Imperial Constitution in 1889 to the present, there arose naturally the difficult problem of what to include and what not to include. This does not purport to be a history of Japan during that period; hence it seemed justifiable to make a general rule of including only those developments which had a direct and immediate reference to the government and its problems. Much that exercised a strong influence, therefore, had to be passed over, as the size of this study was no less restricted than its scope. Such facts, however, are generally available to the student in more truly historical works, some of which are listed in the bibliography following the conclusion.

In editing the manuscript, which, not completely finished, but with notes, was returned with my husband's effects from Shanghai, I have been fortunate in the goodness of my friends. To Professor C. H. Peake of Columbia University I am indebted for some suggestions. Mr. H. M. G. Labatt-Simon of New York City assumed the delicate responsibility of organizing from notes prepared by my husband, those sections which had not been completed. To him I owe my gratitude, particularly for his submergence in the work of another author for which he claims no reward, for without his constant help in editing the entire paper, this study could not have appeared.

My thanks are due, finally, to the publishers, Messrs. Thomas Nelson and Sons, for their patience in receiving a manuscript so long overdue.

JEAN REISCHAUER.

New York City, January 2, 1939.

CONTENTS

INTRODUCTION

INTRODUCTION

IT IS customary today to classify all governments under one of three headings, namely, liberal, fascist, or communist. Yet all these categories are products of only European civilization. In fact, two are primarily little more than different types of reactions against an earlier doctrine of individualism that may have been carried to an extreme by the third. Whatever may be their dissimilarities, they belong to the same stream of civilization, for it is hardly conceivable that fascism and communism, as exemplified in the German, Italian, and Russian regimes, could have developed prior to or apart from the liberal, capitalistic, democratic, individualist European culture of the nineteenth century.

Japan does not belong to this Western stream of civilization. Her government cannot be fitted into any one of these three categories. She has no tradition of liberalism, democracy, capitalism, and individualism. Consequently, she is in no danger of reacting violently against this tradition by turning fascist or communist in an attempt to solve economic and social questions that appear to many Westerners to be insoluble under the rule of liberal political institutions.

The problems that have grown out of the industrial revolution are now beginning to weigh heavily on the minds of Oriental statesmen. They cannot accept any of Europe's three answers of liberalism, fascism, or communism, because their cultural backgrounds are so utterly different from that of the West. It will be interesting to see how Hindus, Chinese, and Japanese try to solve twentieth-century economic and social questions. Japan is the only Oriental power that has progressed far enough industrially to be in dire need of an immediate solution. Many of her leaders feel that in her heritage she possesses one, and they call it not Liberalism, or Fascism, or Communism, but *Kodo*, "The Imperial Way."

In writing about the government of Japan an author cannot take it for granted that the reader possesses that background of information which he brings to the study of the political institutions of almost any Western country. Yet one cannot understand the government that functions according to the principles of "The Imperial Way" unless one first grasps the fundamentals of Japanese political theory, and studies the evolution of the Japanese state from its primitive tribal form into the strongly centralized government that rules the country today.

Surface similarities between European and Japanese political institutions tend only to mislead the Westerner into believing, for example, that the Imperial Japanese Diet is virtually the counterpart of the English Parliament, whereas in reality their bicameral feature is practically the only thing they have in common. Japan's apparently Western governmental organs are little more than a façade that her leaders felt it necessary to erect some fifty years ago in order to win for Japan a status of equality with Occidental powers. If anyone was fooled by this façade, it was the Westerner, not the Japanese. Millions of the sons of *Dai Nippon* know virtually nothing about European political philosophies and institutions, and care even less. It is probably correct to state that the great majority of Japanese who have studied Western governments consider them inferior to their own. A few are enthusiastic over communism, democracy, or fascism. The communists, however, are compelled to keep silent in Japan and to do all their talking in Russia. The fascists usually speak only Japanese or German. It is, therefore, that mere handful of men who are exponents of democracy and liberalism that eulogize Anglo-Saxon political institutions and mores in English to the intense gratification of Americans and Britishers.

Such Japanese do not speak for the real Japan. Most sons of *Dai Nippon* are generally antagonistic toward all "foreign" doctrines. They feel that their country is not in need of learning, but that she has a mission to teach "The Imperial Way" to other nations that are struggling in the morass of communism, democracy, and fascism. Japan has a fourth solution of the grave problems that face the world today. In her opinion "The Imperial Way" is the only true solution.

PART I

JAPANESE POLITICAL THEORY AND GOVERN- MENT

PART I

CHAPTER I

JAPANESE POLITICAL THOUGHT

政 is the Chinese character used in Japan for the concept expressed in English by the word "government." There are significant differences between these two written forms of this single idea. The English word is made up of individual letters, none above or below another, but strung along on a level plane of equality. The letters, whether printed in Roman or Gothic style or written in script, connote by their forms no particular moral values or philosophic ideas. The individual symbols are so loosely held together that one may omit some and have a perfectly good word left, such as "govern" and "men," which in turn can break down into "over" and "me."

In contrast, the Chinese character, although made up of separate strokes, is a single unit. Omit one or more strokes and it is completely ruined. Take enough away and a new ideograph appears; but as all Chinese characters must be the same size, the remnant must be expanded until it fills the old boundaries before it can be accepted as a true character.

Thus there is an interdependence of strokes in Chinese writing not found in the alphabetical languages of the West. In addition, the strokes of the character are classified from left to right, and from top to bottom. Unlike alphabetical letters, some strokes are more important than others, for some must be bold and strong, acting as the pillars of the character, while others can be delicate and graceful. Moreover, in the evolution of Chinese writing, each stroke has come to signify some special philosophical concept. Calligraphy requires such control over the brush that the writing of perfect ideographs has become a method of cultivating virtue; for only the man with calm mind and tranquil heart can write a beautiful Chinese character. Consequently, a perfect 政 displays nuances of moral values and philosophical concepts that are not brought to mind when one sees the English word "government."

In like manner, the main stream of Western political thought tends to emphasize atomic individualism, the equality of all men, and unmoral government, whereas Japanese political thought, due to the legacies of Shinto, Buddhism, and Confucianism, continues to revolve primarily about the community, the inequality of human beings, and the interdependence of politics and ethics. No matter what the detailed machinery of Japanese administration at any time may appear to be, it can be examined and understood only in the light of the traditional Japanese intellectual and emotional attitude toward the business of governing men.

SOCIETY IS MORE IMPORTANT THAN THE INDIVIDUAL

Japanese culture impresses one with a sense of unity, a subordination of parts to a whole, that Euro-

pean civilization has lost since the disintegration of
Catholic Christendom in the Renaissance and the
Reformation. For about five centuries, architecture,
literature, philosophy, science, each realm of knowledge, each field of art has been struggling in the West
to free itself from the control of church and state,
and to declare its independence of all other aspects of
Occidental civilization. The battle cry has been "Art
and Knowledge for Their Own Sake." Consequently,
there have appeared a growing number of deep cleav-
ages in Western culture that have produced today
myriad types of individuals with innumerable stand-
ards of values. Atheists, Catholics, Protestants, Jews,
Liberals, Fascists, Communists, Classicists, Cubists,
Surrealists, and so on without end; and not content
at stopping with the smallest unit, the individual,
there are many who complain, "I feel two natures
struggling within me."

All this is incomprehensible to the true Japanese
who is a Shintoist, a Buddhist, and a Confucianist at
one and the same time; for religion is something indivisible, a tree whose roots may be Shinto, whose
trunk may be Confucianism, and whose fruit and
leaves may be Buddhism and Christianity. Nor, in
his opinion, can religion be separated from politics,
or painting, or the tea ceremony, or the life of a
soldier, or from any aspect of Japanese civilization.
All persons, all arts, all realms of knowledge must be
part and parcel of a single organism. Everything and
every person must be integrated into a single way of
life. For the Japanese believes that the individual
cannot be said to exist except in terms of his contacts
with his fellow men. All life is contained within the
framework of the five Confucian relationships of
ruler and subject, husband and wife, parent and

child, elder child and younger child, friend and friend. The individual is primarily a member of a family and only secondarily an entity in his own right. Moreover, the family is an integral part of a larger unit, the clan, which in turn must subordinate itself to that largest of all families, the whole Japanese nation. It is the belief that almost all the families in Japan are related at least by distant blood ties to the Imperial Family, and hence are but inferior or branch clans of one great nationwide family of which the Emperor is the blood father, that binds the people together in a durable unity so great as to move them to say in all sincerity that "no nation in the world is in a position to vie with Japan in point of the permanency of the State and the solidarity of the people."[1]

Consequently any element that threatens this unity is anathema to the Japanese. It is the emphasis of capitalism on "rugged individualism" and of communism on the "class struggle" that make both hateful to the true Japanese. The idea of *political* parties is also distasteful, for all these things mean a conscious fostering of ideological division and disunity. Japanese disapprove of divided responsibility and always tend to concentrate administrative power in the hands of a few, or preferably one.

It is for this reason that the Emperor plays so great a role in Japanese life. Shinto proclaims him to be the descendant and representative here on earth of the greatest of the Deities of Heaven (*Amatsukami*), the High Priest of his people and their inter-

---

[1] Fujisawa Chikao, *Japanese and Oriental Political Philosophy* (Tokyo, 1935), p. 72. The author is a professor of the Great Oriental Culture College of Tokyo and a member of the Government Research Institute of National Culture. (The customary Japanese style of giving the family name before the personal name is followed here both in text and in citations.)

cessor before the Gods (*Kami*), and finally the blood father or head of the family of which all Japanese are members. Buddhism considers the Emperor a descendant of the supreme Buddha, *Vairoçana,* who manifested himself in Japan as the Great Sun Goddess (*Amaterasu-Omikami*), ancestress of the Imperial Family. He is an incarnation of the eternal and universal Buddha spirit. He is the defender of the faith, the servant of the Three Treasures (*Sam-bo*), consisting of The Buddha, The Law, and The Priesthood. Confucianism maintains that the Emperor is the repository of benevolence, righteousness, and justice. He rules because of his overwhelming virtue. He is the father of his people in the ethical sense, their moral guardian and guide.

So to the Japanese the Emperor is the personification of their unity. A blow struck at him is a blow at all they hold dear, their culture, their very reason for existence; for this sense of unity is the very essence and end of life to the Japanese. Each person must bring his every thought and action into harmony with the principles of "The Imperial Way."

ALL MEN ARE BY NATURE UNEQUAL

To the Japanese, all nature bears silent witness to the doctrine of inequality. No two oceans are equally deep, no two mountains exactly the same size, no two gems equally beautiful, no two animals equally strong. The sun is brighter than the moon, the tortoise slower than the hare. So also among men, some are better than others, some more ethical, more intelligent, and stronger physically than their fellow human beings.

According to Shinto, this inequality among men is based on blood. The Emperor is the Sovereign because he is the most direct descendant of the Sun Goddess. Each subject should have a political and social status commensurate with the nobility of his blood. Those most closely related to the Emperor or descended from the most important Gods (*Kami*) of antiquity should be entitled to greater powers and wealth than those possessing less exalted ancestors.

Confucianism recognizes the fact that there are men of inferior and superior virtue. The latter are quite naturally to be entrusted with the control of the former. It is for them to command, and for the others to obey. "The relationship between superiors and inferiors is like that between the wind and the grass. The grass must bend, when the wind blows across it."[2]

Buddhism accepts present inequalities among men in its doctrines of *karma* and reincarnation. One's life is the reward or punishment for one's past deeds in former incarnations. Consequently, one experiences only what one deserves, no more and no less. If one's *karma* is bad, one must accept the status of a poverty-stricken proletarian with resignation, and not look with envy upon a capitalist who enjoys wealth as a just reward for having created a good *karma* in his former existences.[3]

[2] Chapter 19, Book XII of the Confucian Analects, as translated by James Legge. In James Legge, *The Four Books* (Shanghai, 1930).

[3] It is impossible here to go into any extended discussion of the influences which Shinto, Confucianism, and Buddhism have exercised on Japanese political thought. Instead, a few readings may be suggested in addition to the citations which appear in the present section of this text. For a discussion of Shinto, see D. C. Holtom, *The Political Philosophy of Modern Shinto* (Chicago, 1922). For Confucianism, see R. C. Armstrong, *Light From the East* (Toronto, 1914). There is no authoritative summary of the part Buddhism plays in modern Japanese political philosophy; studies of Buddhism in Japan will be found in Sir Charles Eliot, *Japanese Buddhism* (London, 1935) and in A. K. Reischauer, *Studies in*

The amalgamation of these three hierarchies of Shinto blood, Confucian virtue, and Buddhist *karma* has made the Japanese as aristocratic and class conscious a people as can be found in the annals of history. Yet the Japanese love of unity has prevented these social divisions from destroying the solidarity of the state and Japanese culture. Although the natural inequalities of men make for many classes, each stratum of society is considered to be an integral part of the whole, and its proper functioning is vital to the well-being of the state. The head may control the body, but it is helpless without the other members. The foot need not feel ashamed at not being the heart, for although it is a less vital organ than the other, if it were destroyed the man would cease to be perfect, and would become a cripple. Thus, capitalism because it means the undue oppression of the poorer members of society by the wealthy, and communism because it desires to destroy all classes but one, and finally democracy because it believes in government by all whatever the social status and virtue of its members may be—as though the hands and the feet, because they outnumber the head four to one, should govern the body—are all equally unacceptable to the Japanese.

POLITICS IS SYNONYMOUS WITH ETHICS

Shinto proclaims the Emperor to be the direct descendant of the primary Deity of Heaven (*Amatsukami*), ruling over his people in accordance with the

---

Japanese Buddhism (New York, 1917). As a summary study of religions in Japan, Anesaki Masaharu, *History of Japanese Religion* (Boston, 1930) is useful. If the student is interested to learn a typical contemporary Japanese opinion of the place these religions take in political thought, he might read Fujisawa Chikao, *Japanese and Oriental Political Philosophy* (Tokyo, 1935).

commands of his divine ancestress. He is both King and High Priest. In fact, he is "the Sovereign that is a manifest God."[4] Under such circumstances, no division between "church" and "state" is possible, nor has there ever been such a division in Japanese history.

Confucianism positively will not countenance the divorcing of ethics from government. The universe is run in accordance with the Will of Heaven, or *T'ien*. The affairs of men, being part of the universal order of things, must be regulated in harmony with the commands of Heaven. Only the Philosopher-King is capable of ruling over the people as Heaven desires them to be governed. Thus politics and ethics are mutually interdependent. Government may be moral, or immoral, but never amoral. One may make the distinction in the West between things rendered to Caesar and those to God, but in the Confucian Orient that which is rendered to the Philosopher-King is rendered to Heaven, for the Philosopher-King is Heaven's instrument here on earth. When he fails to be such, he ceases to be the Sovereign.

Buddhism also makes its contribution to this union between the state and religion. It has been consistently looked upon as an instrument of government in Japan. Temples were built, *sûtras* copied and read, and prayers chanted in honor of various Buddhas and Bodhisattvas in order that their spiritual powers would defend Japan and her people from all natural calamities, such as famine, pestilence, and war. The Emperor was looked upon as being a mani-

[4] Sir George Sansom, *Japan: A Short Cultural History* (London, 1932), p. 126. This phrase is Sir George's translation of the Chinese characters used by the Emperor when referring to himself in the imperial edicts of the *Shoku-Nihongi*, a history of Japan covering the years 697-792 A.D.

festation of the universal Buddha spirit. He governed
his people in accordance with the teachings of The
Law in such a manner as to enable his subjects to improve their *karma* so that each might eventually
enter *Nirvana*. Should he fail in his mission, the king-
dom would no longer be ruled in harmony with the
way of the universe, and as a result, calamities and
sorrows would befall the Emperor and his people.

Thus, to govern the state with benevolence and
justice was a sacred duty entrusted by the Great Sun
Goddess of Shinto to "the Sovereign that is a manifest God," by the Spirit of Heaven of Confucianism
to the Philosopher-King, and by the universal
Buddha of Buddhism to the Reincarnation of the
Buddha Spirit. Consequently, it was the function of
government to regulate the lives of its subjects even
to the slightest details of daily existence, for every
action and thought had some permanent effect on the
development of their characters and, as a result, on
their relations with the supernatural.

GOVERNMENT BY MAN IS SUPERIOR TO GOVERNMENT BY LAW

The emphasis of Japanese political philosophy on
unity, inequality, and ethical government has tended
to stress the importance of the officials who draw up
and administer the laws, over and above the laws
themselves. This is due to three reasons.

In the first place, since the individual is looked
upon as being simply a part of the community, it is
unthinkable that he should use the written law as a
sort of bulwark behind which he might defend himself against the encroachments of his government
and his fellow men. That would be an admission that
society is not an indivisible whole, but consists of

many separate units struggling against one another. Laws are not defenses guarding individual rights, but rather ties binding society together. They do not constitute a "Bill of Rights," but a list of one's duties as a member of the national community. These duties are not limited by anything less than the welfare of society as a whole. Consequently, when the rulers decide that the good of the nation demands additional laws or revisions of old ones, changes in legislation are made with but slight regard to the differences these will make in the political and economic status of the people thereby affected. Written law is not something permanent, guaranteeing rights and privileges to individuals, but simply a temporary expression of the opinion of the official class as to what is good for the nation at a given moment.

In the second place, since Japanese emphasis on inequality divides society rather definitely into the governors and the governed, laws are put into written form not so much in order to enable the individual subject to ascertain the minimum number of duties his rulers expect him to perform and just what line of conduct he may pursue without running afoul of the authorities, but primarily in order that the officials may have a convenient method of procedure to follow in governing, and a relatively consistent standard whereby they may rule the people. In the past it was not thought wise to let the common man always know the law, for it was argued that a knowledge of the written law simply made him lawless. Once he knew exactly what was the law, he would bend all his efforts to circumvent it. As long as he was ignorant of its exact wording and was simply informed about its general principles, he would strive to lead as righteous a life as he knew how for fear that he might be breaking the law and consequently displeasing the authorities. Because it was believed that officials were men of superior virtue, it was taken for granted that they would rule justly; that when the common subject broke the law unwittingly they would decide when punishment was advisable and when it could be safely waived.

In the third place, since government must be moral, since the foundation of an ethical administration is the cultivation of the personal integrity of each individual official, and since the ruling class is supposed to consist of men of superior virtue, it is felt that the governors are superior to the law. A written law is simply an expression of the opinion of certain rulers at a given time concerning a specific subject. But conditions are never exactly the same twice. The law is rigid and inflexible. The official, however, being a man of superior virtue, has a conscience that is often a far better guide than the written law, because the conscience is not bound by time and place and a given set of phenomena as is the law. Consequently, the official is not to be limited in the exercise of his duty by existing legislation. He is to look upon the law simply as a convenient embodiment of certain principles. His interpretation of it, even to the point of virtually disobeying the law, must be governed by the peculiar circumstances of each individual case. He must follow his conscience as his guide. This is the only way to make certain that true justice will be rendered at all times.

Thus the Japanese have laid great stress on personalities in government and have paid less attention to form, theory, and law. It is the officials themselves that make a government either just or tyrannical. It is not the organization of the state, but the governing class; not the political theory, but the men who put that theory into practice; not the laws, but the officials who create and enforce them that are important. A good Confucianist cannot become particularly interested in the various "isms" and "ocracies" for which so many Westerners have been willing even to lay down their lives. Socialism, communism, fascism, anarchism, capitalism, democracy, autocracy, and the rest are simply words to him. Why get excited about such intangible things? How many people can agree as to what they really mean? Back of those words lie the men. They and they alone are important. As Confucius states in "The Doctrine of the Mean": "Let there be the men and the government will flourish; but without the men, their government decays and ceases. With the right men the growth of government is rapid. . . . Therefore the administration of government lies in getting proper men . . ."[5] Quibbling over the problems of sovereignty, citizenship, law, the state, and so forth may be excellent intellectual gymnastics, and political theory unquestionably has had a profound influence on the development of political institutions, but whatever the underlying theory, the personalities and characters of the men who interpret it and put it into practice determine whether the application of that particular theory will bring happiness or misery to the people. It is the officials, not the law, that will save or destroy the state.

THE PATRIARCHAL FAMILY IS THE IDEAL STATE

It must now be evident to the reader why the patriarchal family is the ideal state. In such a family

[5] "The Doctrine of the Mean" (Legge's translation) Ch. XX, Sec. 2, 3, 4. In James Legge, *The Four Books* (Shanghai, 1930).

the individual subordinates his life to the good of the whole. No two members have the same status in the family councils, for they are rigidly stratified according to sex, degree of kinship to the head of the clan, age, and prestige. Yet whatever the differences in importance and power, no attempt of one to deprive another of his rights is tolerated. However small and unimportant may be her share in the life of the family, only the second daughter can fill the second daughter's position. The clan is governed according to accepted mores. The same standard of ethics applies to all phases of the communal life. The patriarch and the elders of the family council are acknowledged as superiors in virtue and experience to the rank and file of the clan. They are trusted to rule justly and to show mercy. Their governance will not be strictly legal and coldly impersonal, but equitable. Their policy will be to fit the punishment to the crime after taking all personal factors into consideration.

It is stated time and again in Japanese political writings that the state is simply a gigantic patriarchal family. The Emperor is the adored father, the revered statesmen are the council of clan elders, and the people are the children, some having more honorable positions than others, but each being treated according to his due, all being cared for as beloved and homogeneous members of a single great family. That the Japanese people are the obedient and loving children of their fathers, the Sovereigns, and rejoice that they are so wisely "governed by a line of Emperors unbroken for ages eternal"[6] is the fundamental doctrine of "The Imperial Way."

[6] From the first article of the Imperial Constitution of 1889.

INTERNATIONAL ASPECTS OF JAPANESE POLITICAL PHILOSOPHY

The Japanese sense of unity makes them conscious of humanity as an indivisible whole. But whereas this feeling in the West has given rise to the international spirit, such has not been the case in Japan. For internationalism, as the word implies, means an association of separate, sovereign states. There again rises the specter of Western individualism. The Japanese desire a community of nations in which the individual parts would be subordinated to the good of the whole, although this would mean the rigid curtailment of the sovereignty of perhaps all the states.

Because of their belief in inequality, however, the Japanese feel that although all the states of the world should be bound together in the exercise of a universal sovereignty, in practice this sovereignty must be wielded only by the state best fitted to govern. The Philosopher-King nation must assume the main responsibility for ushering in the age of international peace and justice.

Among nations, the Philosopher-King is the one that realizes that politics is synonymous with ethics, that to govern is to do the will of Heaven. Fascism makes a god of the totalitarian state; communism is avowedly atheistic and enthrones the proletariat; and liberalism proclaims the generality of citizens, however lacking they may be in virtue and intelligence, to be the arbiters of politics and ethics. The energies of all three are misdirected, and need redirecting. Thus it is only the nation that follows "The Imperial Way" that is worthy to exercise universal sovereignty. Hence, "Japan is the sole nation qualified to convey to the world the blessings of the

Way of the Sage-King, and on the realization of this ideal, mental equilibrium and moral calm will be restored to afflicted humanity."[7]

Should some question the advisability of entrusting the fate of the world to a nation whose reputation for observing its written international commitments is as poor as is Japan's at present, it must be remembered the Japanese believe that government by man is superior to government by law. What is known as the doctrine of *rebus sic stantibus* in the West is an integral part of Japanese political theory. The Sovereign, functioning through the Imperial Japanese Government, may deign to place his signature on a treaty, because at that given moment that written document is an expression of his will. But should circumstances be altered considerably, or should he simply change his mind, the Japanese cannot see why they are to be accused of bad faith merely because they disregard the treaty and adopt a different policy from the one they had pledged themselves at some former date to pursue. Just as domestic laws are but a statement of government opinion on a specific matter at a given moment, so also Japan's international commitments are simply statements of foreign policy at the time the treaty is signed. Internally the government has no compunction about breaking its written contracts with individual subjects or corporations whenever domestic policy is served thereby. Externally the Imperial Japanese Government abrogates international treaties unilaterally with but little compunction. Man is superior to law. He is its originator and destroyer, not its abject slave.

[7] Fujisawa, *Japanese and Oriental Political Philosophy*, cited, p. 169.

CRITICISM OF JAPANESE POLITICAL THOUGHT

This philosophy, however, fails to take into account the human nature of the very men whom it places above the law. Thus Japan has never been that paradise of benevolence and justice which Japanese political thought and its present-day exponents depict for the Western world. The governing class developed an excellent technique of making use of every last drop of loyalty it could wring from the common people, but too often it betrayed this devotion. Shinto emphasis on ancestry tended to concentrate political, economic, and social privileges in the hands of a closed aristocracy that grew progressively more self-satisfied, more grasping, and more incompetent until it destroyed itself time and again by its own weakness and corruption. The confidence of Confucianism in the natural goodness of man, with the corresponding lack of that deep sense of sin or of failure to live up to one's highest ideals, and Confucian emphasis on the aristocracy of virtue, tended to make the governing class smugly complacent, loudly stressing the duties of inferiors to be filial and loyal, while speaking *pianissimo* about the concomitant responsibilities of superiors to be benevolent and just. Buddhist other-worldliness made those in authority who enjoyed comfortable existences because of their high status in society, view with a great deal of equanimity and unconcern the temporary this-worldly miseries of the less fortunate. Worldly existence was held to be an illusion and man's life was the result only of his *karma*. Although something might be said for improving the pitiable conditions of the lower classes, arguments to the contrary were perhaps equally valid, for according to Buddhist concepts of knowledge and truth, "Contradictions become but two sides of the same thing, and from this viewpoint a system with the greatest contradictions is *ipso facto* the most comprehensive statement of the full truth."[8]

But it was the idea of government by man rather than government by law that had the most baleful influence on Japanese history. Confucius had argued that the men of superior virtue ought to be the officials, but in actual practice it was frequently quite the contrary.[9] The leveling influence of examinations open to candidates from all social classes, which generally operated in China, never survived the rigid barriers by which the Japanese aristocracy surrounded itself. When unscrupulous men were in power there was no way that the common man had of protecting himself from their tyranny, for officials were frequently, in practice, above the law. Instead of being considered the fathers of their people, such officials were more often likened to beasts of prey. Men of integrity and ability often found they had to retire from politics if they would save their lives, for higher officials would not hesitate to effect their destruction. This meant that when government started to become corrupt, it went rapidly from bad to worse until the resulting chaos destroyed the men in power who produced it.

THE INFLUENCE OF WESTERN POLITICAL THEORIES

Japan was in just such a state of social and economic confusion when Commodore Perry forced open

[8] August Karl Reischauer, *Studies in Japanese Buddhism* (New York, 1917), p. 321.
[9] See Lin Yutang's book, *My Country and My People* (New York, 1936) for a bitter denunciation of Confucianism as a political philosophy.

the islands to occidental culture in 1853. Chinese civilization was thoroughly discredited at the moment, and influential groups were ready for some change in the *status quo*. Eager to make their country powerful, so that Japan might be able to preserve her political independence, the leaders of the new imperial regime that overthrew the Tokugawa Shogunate and feudalism sought a reason for the Westerner's military strength and his great economic wealth, and some believed they had discovered a clue to it in his democratic political institutions. In a very short time liberal Japanese who had traveled to the West and had been intrigued by occidental ways were talking glibly about *liberté, egalité, fraternité*, the social contract theory, *laissez faire*, individualism, and were reading avidly the works of Bentham, Montesquieu, Rousseau, Voltaire, the Mills, Spencer, and a host of other political writers. The demands for some sort of representative, constitutional government became so vehement that it was deemed wise by the ruling clique to have the Emperor issue an Imperial Decree in 1881, promising the establishment of an Imperial Diet in 1890. After the World War and the Russian Revolution, even socialism and communism became immensely popular among the young intellectuals.

However, from time to time would come a wave of reaction brought on either by anger at something done by a Western power, or by worry over the social and economic problems raised in Japan by the coming of the Industrial Revolution. The people would then turn to the rabid chauvinists of old Japan for their inspiration, or read with enthusiasm the nationalistic writings of Germans such as Hegel. Recently, the birth of fascism, coupled with the movement

toward economic nationalism growing out of the
world depression, has so strengthened this reactionary group that since 1931 Japan has been experienc-
ing a very severe case of antiforeign feeling.[10]

It is still too early to prophesy the result during
the next few decades of the impact of Western political thought on the organization of the Japanese
state. The old theories of government are no longer
intellectually satisfying to a growing number of modern Japanese, nor do they prove capable of application to twentieth-century *Nippon*. On the other
hand, the new doctrines of communism, liberalism,
and fascism, evolved by peoples of wholly different
historical backgrounds, have not fitted the situation
peculiar to Japan. The prophets of "The Imperial
Way" proclaim that its teachings remain true to
Japanese traditions while adapting them to modern
conditions, thereby furnishing the people a way of
life that is both historically and psychologically acceptable and yet which meets and solves the problems of present-day *Nippon*. Unfortunately, the average Japanese is still quite vague as to just what
"The Imperial Way" is, and until its doctrines have
been better defined and explained, the future course
of Japanese politics will remain unpredictable.

[10] It is true that this antiforeign feeling, directed at the more
democratic nations, has been accompanied by a diplomatic alignment with the fascist powers; but this may be more the result of
Japan's overwhelming sense of need for defense against Russia and
communism than of an active liking for Germans and Italians in
the face of a hostility toward England and France.

CHAPTER II

THE EVOLUTION OF THE JAPANESE GOVERNMENT

JAPAN is a mountainous country with a topography that proved admirably suited in antiquity to the growth of many small, independent tribal states. The chieftains were called *Uji-no-kami*, each ruling over his own clan (*uji*). Their positions were hereditary, for each claimed descent from some Deity of Heaven (*Amatsu-kami*) or Deity of Earth (*Kunitsu-kami*), and his main function was to supervise the sacrifices to his divine ancestor, the Clan Deity (*Uji-gami*), in order that through the resulting good will of this potent spirit peace and prosperity might be visited upon the whole clan. All the clansmen (*uji-bito*) were descended from this same Clan Deity and hence were related by blood ties to the Clan Chieftain. It was considered so important that the Clan Deity be worshiped by the most direct descendant that the Clan Chieftain frequently married a half-sister in order to conserve the blood inheritance as much as possible. Beneath the clansmen were hereditary corporations (*be*) of farmers and artisans who were the economic backbone of society, and below them were the slaves (*nuhi*). These people were generally conquered aborigines, prisoners of war, immigrants from the continent, or criminals. Among these only the criminals came from the blood relationship of the clan, nor was there any opportunity for the others to enter the close caste of the clansmen. This was Shinto society in its simplest and purest form.

A PRIMITIVE TRIBAL THEOCRACY
(?–7TH CENTURY A.D.)[1]

Among the many hundreds of small, independent tribal kingdoms of ancient Japan was one located in the fertile and strategic region that was later to be the site of the great cities of Nara, Kyoto, and Osaka. Its Clan Chieftain traced his ancestry to the Great Sun Goddess, *Amaterasu-Omikami*. In time, as this clan was able to extend its political sway over surrounding tribes, the other Clan Deities were assigned definite places in a Shinto pantheon in which the Sun Goddess was given the central position as the supreme Deity of Heaven (*Amatsu-kami*). Those that could not be fitted into this hierarchy in Heaven were declared Deities of Earth (*Kunitsu-kami*), who were, however, considered to be descendants of the Deities of Heaven. The Clan Chieftains who claimed the Sun Goddess as their ancestress found it politic to evolve a genealogy that made them related through their maternal ancestors to most of the other important Deities of Heaven and Earth and thereby related to the Clan Chieftains of the other great clans. Gradually, they became so powerful that the other Clan Chieftains had to render them service in one capacity or another, becoming secular or sacerdotal, civil or military officials of the rising centralized Clan State. These official posts were hereditary, the object being to establish here on earth a replica of the hierarchy of Deities existing in Heaven, although in actual fact it was really the early power of the Clan Chieftains

[1] For a full treatment of this subject see Robert Karl Reischauer, *Early Japanese History (c. 40 B.C.—A.D. 1167)* (Princeton, 1937).

and their clansmen that first determined the status of their ancestral Clan Deities (*Uji-gami*) in the Shinto pantheon.

Through growing contact with Chinese civilization, society became more complex, and as a result more advanced types of political institutions were evolved.[2] The powerful direct descendant of the Sun Goddess began to consider himself a sort of "King" or "Emperor." As the central group of clans increased their control over the rest of Japan, Local Chieftains (*Kuni-no-miyatsuko*) who had charge over the various hereditary corporations (*be*) belonging to the "Imperial Family" were increased. With the growing concentration of economic wealth and political power at the "Imperial Court," the great clans closely related to the "Imperial Family" began to grow dangerously strong. While several rival clans remained powerful, there was no particular threat to the position of the "Emperor," but on the overthrow of one clan after another in the bitter political struggles that took place, the "Emperors" came to be puppets in the hands of victorious clan factions.

The sophistication of Confucianism and Buddhism was undermining the primitive Shinto faith on which the loyalty of the clans was based. The "Emperor" and the Clan Chieftains found they had to rely increasingly on their military and economic powers as their sacerdotal influence waned. Upstarts were brazenly faking their genealogies. The flood of immigrants from the continent and large migrations of people within Japan due to the increase of the popu-

---

[2] Although it is not a recent book, Asakawa Kanichi, *The Early Institutional Life of Japan* (Tokyo, 1903) is still the best treatment of this period.

lation, threw the whole clan system of government based on blood ties into confusion. The bonds of place were proving more important than the bonds of family to unite various groups in Japanese society. In short, Chinese civilization was making life so much more complex that the old political institutions had outgrown their usefulness. A far more centralized and efficient form of government had to be established. The time was ripe for great changes.

Nevertheless, these early centuries of primitive Shinto society had left so permanent an imprint on Japanese culture that whatever forms the new political institutions might take, they would have to accept the basic Shinto principle of an aristocracy of blood. Whatever the new officials might be called and whatever their duties might be, their posts would have to be, to a very great extent, hereditary. That Shinto emphasis on ancestry did survive all changes in Japanese history is proved conclusively by the fact that the present Emperor is regarded as a direct descendant of the Great Sun Goddess. Moreover, Prince Saionji, last of the Elder Statesmen or *Genro*, and Prince Konoe, Premier of Japan, are both believed to be descendants in the main line of the Heavenly Deity, *Ame-no-Koyane-no-Mikoto,* who recited Shinto liturgies (*norito*) before the Sun Goddess in Heaven, who accompanied the Imperial Grandson on his journey down to earth to found the Japanese Empire, and whose descendants established the great Nakatomi clan, the hereditary chieftains of which served generation after generation as the highest Shinto sacerdotal officials at the "Imperial Court" in this early period of the primitive, tribal, theocratic state.

A BUREAUCRATIC, CIVIL ARISTOCRACY
(7TH–12TH CENTURIES)

The Chinese Empire of the seventh century under the great T'ang Emperors was probably the most prosperous and best-governed state of its time in the world. The ruling class of Japan, searching for a political system that would strengthen its weakening hold on the common people and that would raise its standard of living, inevitably turned to China for guidance. As a result, a serious attempt was made to transplant Chinese institutions into Japan.

The powerful Clan Chieftain who claimed direct descent from the Great Sun Goddess, but who was only *primus inter pares*, now ascended to the dazzling political height of an Emperor. He became "The One Man," "The Supreme Monarch." All land became his land, all people his direct subjects. Primitive tribal institutions were supplanted by a highly centralized and complicated bureaucracy. The various Clan Chieftains became important officials of the new empire. Since the Chinese plan called for the choice of officials according to a merit system based on examinations on the Confucian Classics, men with political ambitions forsook military arts in favor of literary pursuits. The governing class became distinctly civil in character.

The Japanese were not blind imitators, however, but made some changes in their new Chinese institutions in order to adapt them to the political, social, and economic conditions peculiar to Japan. These changes are of great significance, for in time they proved so fundamental as to make impossible the proper functioning of these new institutions. Within two centuries the similarity between Chinese and

Japanese forms of government became mostly super-ficial. Those Westerners who have a tendency to stress the resemblance between modern Japanese governmental organs and the occidental originals after which they were patterned would do well to remember this fate of Chinese political institutions in Japan during the seventh, eighth, and ninth centuries.

The aristocratic Shinto emphasis on blood, which was inherited from the period of the primitive, tribal, theocratic state, proved stronger than the relatively democratic Confucian emphasis on virtue. The Japanese never accepted the Chinese doctrine that the Emperor rules because of his supreme virtue, and that the people have the right to rebel when the Emperor has lost this virtue and hence no longer rules in accordance with the Will of Heaven. If virtue has anything to do with sovereignty, then the Japanese Emperor, because he is the most direct descendant of the Great Sun Goddess, who undoubtedly would not have been the Ruler of Heaven unless she had been the most virtuous of all the Deities, always inherits this superior virtue from his divine ancestress and remains forever the most virtuous person on earth. Hence, no right to rebel was ever recognized. That is one reason why there have been many dynasties in China and but one in Japan.

Moreover, the Chinese practice of appointing officials on the basis of merit as ascertained in examinations was too democratic a method for Japanese to accept. They observed the letter of the law, but destroyed its spirit by permitting only members of a certain social status to take the examinations. In a relatively short time all important posts in the civil bureaucracy became hereditary once more. This bred increasing inefficiency in the administration and drove ambitious members of lesser families to seek their fortunes as military men in the provinces, thereby contributing greatly to the breakdown of the central government and the rise of feudalism.

The main branch of the great Nakatomi clan that had played so important a role in sacerdotal affairs in earlier times, had changed its name to Fujiwara. This family became so powerful that its heads became Civil Dictators (*Kampaku*) of Japan, and its lesser members usurped all the high positions in the government. The Emperors were reduced to the status of puppets and were permitted to marry only women of the Fujiwara clan, being promptly removed from the throne as soon as these ladies had borne sons that could be controlled as infant sovereigns by their maternal grandfathers, the Civil Dictators.[3] The Emperors retained the exercise of their duties as high priests of their people, but ceased to be responsible for the conduct of temporal affairs.

Thus was established in the years from the seventh to the twelfth centuries the firm tradition that the Emperor reigns, but does not rule, delegating his powers to various hereditary officials of a bureaucratic, civil aristocracy that controls the people in the interests of its own closed caste. The basis of sovereignty was still theocratic, but the exercise of it was now vested in a civil bureaucracy composed of hereditary officials chosen from a very few noble families.

[3] The reader is reminded that Prince Saionji, the last of the Elder Statesmen or *Genro*, and Prince Konoe, the present premier of Japan, are direct descendants of these Civil Dictators.

A MILITARY ARISTOCRACY (12TH–15TH CENTURIES)

A centralized, bureaucratic government can function properly only so long as its officials are reasonably capable and its financial status is fairly satisfactory. However, as political posts became hereditary in Japan, inefficiency became the order of the day. Moreover, these officials were paid for their services in terms of grants of land and of farming households. These were not considered private property at first and had to be returned to the state on the expiration of one's term of office. But when the same posts became hereditary in certain families, these grants of land soon turned into private manors (*shoen*) and the grants of farming households into serfs belonging to their masters and no longer direct subjects of the crown. As the population increased, additional land had to be brought under cultivation. Those who already owned private estates and serfs had the necessary capital to invest in such undertakings, so that they were able to increase their personal holdings. Being officials in the government, they passed laws freeing their lands and serfs from the payment of all forms of taxation, and even forbade the entrance of any imperial officials into their private manors. Thus grew up a group of little states within the imperial realm.[4]

Deprived of its sources of revenue, the central government gradually ceased to be able to maintain law and order in the provinces. The local landholders then had to furnish their own police and soldiers. This gave rise to a military class of warriors (*bushi*)

[4] For a fuller discussion of this manorial system, see Robert Karl Reischauer, "The Japanese *Shoen* or Manor," *Journal of the American Oriental Society,* Vol. 57, No. 1.

later known as the *samurai*. By the close of the
twelfth century the bureaucratic, civil aristocracy
had lost control of the situation and power had gravi-
tated into the hands of a hereditary local gentry
whose strength lay in its fighting men. The greatest
of these provincial landholders and warriors had the
Emperor appoint him Military Dictator, or *Shogun*,
and placed his most trusted retainers as Military
Protectors (*Shugo*) and Land Stewards (*Jito*) in
strategic localities throughout the country. Thus was
born a military aristocracy.

Thereafter Japan had a dual form of government.
Although the Emperor still officiated as the high
priest of his people and the civil bureaucracy composed of nobles from the Fujiwara family exercised
sovereignty in his name in civil matters pertaining
to education, customs, etiquette, and so forth, all
military affairs, including the maintenance of law
and order, were now entrusted to the Military Dictator. It was inevitable that the two aristocracies, the
civil and the military, should have come to blows
over the question of their relative spheres of influence, and that the military aristocracy, because of its
superior power, should have won time and time
again, steadily limiting the importance and scope of
the functions of the civil bureaucracy until it had
lost virtually all control over the affairs of state.[5]

These centuries from the twelfth to the fifteenth,
therefore, witnessed the third stage in the evolution
of the Japanese Government. The basis of sovereignty was still theocratic. The Emperor still offi-

[5] The Imperial Court never completely lost the control of foreign affairs. It became the power of the *Shogun* to decide with
whom relations should be maintained, and with what intentions,
as a corollary power to the responsibility of national defense. But
the deciding voice in diplomacy never left the Court.

ciated in his sacerdotal capacity as the high priest of his people. A bureaucratic, civil aristocracy still exercised that sovereignty, but within steadily diminishing bounds. A new military aristocracy had appeared, however, which ruled the country through a Military Dictator, or *Shogun*. Although his appointment derived from the Emperor, this had become a mere form since the Emperor was powerless to exercise any choice in the matter. The civil aristocracy had been shorn of practically all power. The hereditary Military Protectors and Land Stewards had become local magnates over whom even the Military Dictators could no longer exercise complete control. Japan was now definitely in her age of feudalism.

THE RISE OF THE BOURGEOISIE
(15TH–19TH CENTURIES)

Just as government by the Court Nobles (*Kuge*) of the bureaucratic, civil aristocracy foundered on the rocks of hereditary officialdom and the disappearance of the public domain, so in turn the military aristocracy under the Military Dictators (*Shogun*) was wrecked for a time by the growing lawlessness of the Military Protectors (*Shugo*) and Land Stewards (*Jito*) who began to throw off their allegiance to the central military bureaucracy and to become independent Feudal Barons (*Buke*). The private manors (*shoen*) that had begun to appear as early as the eighth century definitely became feudal fiefs by the close of the fifteenth century.

In the political confusion that increased as government became more decentralized, much of the old civil aristocracy of the Court Nobles (*Kuge*) was destroyed, and many of the great clans of the military aristocracy of the Feudal Barons (*Buke*) were completely wiped out, so that there was a large influx of new blood into the top stratum of society. What is of even greater significance, however, is that with the rise of many independent political centers under ambitious territorial barons, each of whom was eager to increase his political sphere of influence and his economic wealth, a great impetus was given to the improvement of means of communication and transportation, and to the promotion of trade, both domestic and foreign. Powerful merchant guilds (*za*) consequently came into existence. These were able to win various privileges from the Feudal Barons who needed their economic support. The merchant guilds of the important seaport of Sakai, located just south of the present great manufacturing city of Osaka, became so strong that their mercenary troops made Sakai a free city independent of all Feudal Barons, and governed by a council of city elders chosen from among the wealthiest business men.[6]

Not only did the bourgeoisie make their first appearance during these centuries as a political power, but the status of the whole farming class was raised by its increasing military importance to the Feudal Barons. The lack of any strong central administration meant that each local potentate had to keep a large standing army ready for any emergency. The introduction of firearms by the Portuguese in the middle of the sixteenth century[7] revolutionized the art of warfare and made any common farmer a potential musketeer and hence of fighting value to his overlord. The number of farmers who were therefore incor-

[6] For this and economic developments of the bourgeoisie generally see Takekoshi Yosaburo, *Economic Aspects of the History of the Civilization of Japan.* (Tokyo, 1930), 3 vols.

[7] The exact date is debatable. It was, however, probably not more than two years before or after 1543.

porated as light troops (*ashigaru*) in the feudal armies increased tremendously. This gave them not only a new feeling of self-respect, but also the means whereby to protect themselves from too great exploitation. Consequently, the number and severity of peasant rebellions increased in the fifteenth and sixteenth centuries. The Feudal Barons found they had to grant more and more local autonomy to the villages and pay more respect to the rights of the farmers, if they were to obtain their economic and military co-operation in the incessant feudal wars.

In this manner, and for these reasons, there appeared the beginnings of a middle class movement toward establishing representative political institutions. The bourgeoisie in the free and semifree towns acquired a taste for political independence, while in the thousands of little country villages, the peasants won for themselves a degree of local autonomy and freedom from control by the warrior (*bushi*) class never before enjoyed by the mass of ordinary farmers.

The centrifugal forces that had operated to destroy first the civil and then the military aristocracies and to bring into existence a centralized feudalism were largely spent by the latter half of the sixteenth century. Already a centripetal movement had begun, this being based primarily on an improvement in the methods of transportation and communication, the expansion of trade, the growth of towns, the increasing economic interdependence of the several parts of Japan, the gradual change from a barter to a money economy, the growth in size and power of the feudal armies, the decreasing value of feudal fortifications because of the introduction of cannons, and the rising popular demand for peace at almost any price after so many decades of war and political chaos.

This trend of the times made possible the growth of large feudal states, such as that of the Shimazu family of Satsuma and the Mori family of Choshu, and finally brought about the unification of Japan under Tokugawa Ieyasu. This great feudal baron and his allies were able in 1600 to crush all opposition. In 1603 he was proclaimed Military Dictator, or *Shogun*, by the Emperor, thereby founding the Tokugawa Shogunate which was to last for over two hundred and fifty years until 1867.

Tokugawa Ieyasu and his successors ruled Japan as *Shogun* from their castle in Edo, the old name for Tokyo. Approximately one-fourth of the country, including practically every important city and seaport, belonged to the *Shogun*. All this territory was governed directly by the feudal bureaucracy set up by the Tokugawa family. Posts in this government were open only to lords (*daimyo*) and knights (*samurai*) who were hereditary vassals of the *Shogun*. All other Feudal Barons and their warriors were excluded.

The remaining three-fourths of Japan was divided among the great lords (*daimyo*), about half being held by hereditary vassals and branch families of the Tokugawa, while approximately half was controlled by "outer-lords" (*tozama-daimyo*), such as the Shimazu of Satsuma, the Mori of Choshu, the Nabeshima of Hizen, and the Yamanouchi of Tosa. These latter *daimyo* were looked upon as potential enemies of the Tokugawa family. Consequently, to keep them and their *samurai* under control, the Tokugawa Shogunate not only excluded them from all posts in the administration but compelled the *daimyo* to spend every other year in attendance on the *Shogun* at Edo, to leave their wives and children as hostages permanently at Edo, to make no alliances among themselves, to have no contacts with the Emperor and the Court Nobles (*Kuge*) in Kyoto, and to engage in no relations with foreign countries except with the permission of the central authorities. In return for this submission, the Tokugawa family did not meddle with the internal affairs of the various feudal states, only interfering when the peace was disturbed.

This system of centralized feudalism could function only if the Tokugawa Shogunate was able to maintain its position of predominance, or in other words, only if it could maintain the *status quo*. Hence it bent every effort toward this end. The country had to be closed to all foreign intercourse to remove the possibility that some ambitious *daimyo* who might wish to rebel against the central government could obtain outside assistance. Since the *Shogun's* power depended on the support of his hereditary Feudal Barons and their warriors, the administration did all it could to strengthen and make permanent the superior political, economic, and social status enjoyed by the *samurai*. Class lines were drawn rigidly. Farmers were looked upon as being simply taxable objects, and the townspeople were considered parasites on society, neither fighting to preserve it as did the warriors, nor working to enrich it by the production of staples as did the farmers. Consequently, the bourgeoisie were relegated to the bottom of the social scale and at best were scarcely tolerated.

Despite all the precautions the Tokugawa Shogunate took to maintain itself in power permanently, it collapsed shortly after the middle of the nineteenth century. This was not due primarily to outside pressure as a result of Commodore Perry's opening of Japan in 1853; it was more significant that the *status quo* had not been maintained within the country. The Tokugawa family had believed itself secure so long as it kept its rivals, the outer-lords (*tozama-daimyo*), weak and disunited. It had never imagined that the whole feudal aristocracy, including the Tokugawa family, might be destroyed by some other group. Yet precisely that happened.

The two hundred and fifty years of peace that followed the establishment of a system of centralized feudalism in 1603 witnessed the slow but steady change from a barter to a money economy. The financial structure of the Tokugawa Shogunate was based on rice. The incomes of the Tokugawa family, of all the *daimyo* and their *samurai*, were computed in terms of so many *koku* of rice,[8] for that had been the standard commodity of exchange at the opening of the seventeenth century. Peace and centralization of political power, however, brought with them a great development of commerce and industry. Osaka became the economic capital of a national economy, as Edo had become the political capital of a centralized feudalism. All the *daimyo* were compelled to maintain large permanent establishments at Edo, and to undertake the long journey thither from their fiefs every other year. Rice was too bulky a commodity to carry in large amounts all over the country. The influx of a large quantity of coins from China and the encouragement given to mining of precious metals and the minting of coins in Japan soon produced a situation in which money supplanted rice as the ordinary means of exchange. The *daimyo* and their *samurai* were forced to transport their rice to Osaka for

[8] 1 Koku = 5.11 dry American bushels.

sale there in order to convert rice salaries into specie before they could purchase everyday commodities.

This brought about the rise of a group of rice merchants and money changers who were all recruited from the despised class of townspeople. These men promptly began to reap fabulous fortunes by manipulating rice prices, demanding large sums for converting rice into money, and by charging exorbitant interest rates on the loans they made to *daimyo* and their *samurai*. Whereas the standard and the cost of living rose continuously throughout the Tokugawa era, the price of rice not only fluctuated violently whenever there were floods, droughts, or bumper crops, but also tended on the whole to decline in relation to other commodity prices, despite all the frantic attempts of the government to stabilize it at a relatively high level. As a consequence, the feudal class, almost to a man, lived above its income, so that it was estimated that even by 1730 the total debts of the *daimyo* to the merchant class were a hundred times as great as all the cash in the country; and by 1850 it was stated that about fifteen-sixteenths of all the property of the Feudal Barons and their *samurai* was mortgaged to the despised townspeople.[9]

When Commodore Perry came to Japan in 1853, the Tokugawa Shogunate was virtually bankrupt. Almost all the great *daimyo* were hopelessly in debt and their *samurai* were living in real poverty. Hordes of lordless warriors known as *ronin*, who had been dismissed by their superiors in order to reduce expenses, were without permanent means of support and hence

[9] Much of this material is taken from Takigawa Masajiro's excellent work entitled *Nihon-shakai-shi* (*Social History of Japan*) (Tokyo, 1935). Those who are unable to read Japanese are advised to read Honjo Eijiro, *The Social and Economic History of Japan* (Kyoto, 1935).

eager for any sort of change. Agrarian Japan was being taxed to the limit in a vain attempt to rescue the feudal lords from their burden of debts, while the despised bourgeoisie were growing stronger in numbers and in wealth every day and were becoming increasingly desirous of winning social and political recognition from the ruling class. In most of the feudal fiefs the *daimyo* had become mere puppets in the hands of enterprising subordinates who were disgusted with the social order and the existing economic situation. These lesser *samurai* and all the other groups who were dissatisfied with the feudal regime were gathering about the Emperor as a focal point. The inability of the Shogunate to deal satisfactorily with European and American powers, and as a result, the imminent danger of political extinction in which Japan found itself, furnished the opponents of the Edo authorities an excellent excuse for insisting on the dissolution of the Tokugawa feudal government. Consequently, in 1867 the opposition forces demanded the abdication of the *Shogun* and the "restoration" of the Emperor. Under the military leadership of the powerful Shimazu clan of Satsuma and the Mori clan of Choshu, with the support of other great feudal barons such as the Nabeshima family of Hizen and the Yamanouchi family of Tosa, and Court Nobles (*Kuge*) such as the Saionji, Konoe, Sanjo, and Tokudaiji families, and financed by the great mercantile houses of Osaka, such as the Mitsui, the imperial forces were able to overthrow the centralized feudal regime of the Tokugawa *Shogun* and bring about the so-called Meiji Restoration.

CHAPTER III

THE ESTABLISHMENT OF A CONSTITUTIONAL GOVERNMENT
(1867–1889)

In 1867, with the support of the three other powerful outer-lords (*tozama-daimyo*) of western Japan—Lords Shimazu of Satsuma, Mori of Choshu, and Nabeshima of Hizen—Lord Yamanouchi of Tosa demanded that the Tokugawa *Shogun* resign and return all power to the Emperor. Since two of the strongest branch families of the Tokugawa clan, the *Daimyo* of Owari and Echizen, supported this order, the last of the *Shogun* complied, and with some relief transferred the burdens of state affairs to the shoulders of the Emperor. Being still by far the wealthiest and most powerful *daimyo* in Japan, he expected that he would undoubtedly serve as the highest official under the new regime.

Such was not the intention, however, of the leaders of the restoration movement: Sanjo Saneyoshi—an old enemy of the Shogunate—and Iwakura Tomoyoshi, members of the Court Nobility (*Kuge*); Saigo Takamori and Okubo Toshimichi, two important *samurai* of Lord Shimazu of Satsuma; and Kido Koin—the man most responsible for bringing about the coalition of the four great Western clans—a *samurai* of Lord Mori of Choshu. Impelled by loyalty to the Emperor, hatred of the Tokugawa family for its two hundred and fifty years of tyranny over the Court Nobles and the outer-lords, and personal am-

bitions, these men were bent on destroying utterly
the power of the *ex-Shogun* and his loyal hereditary
lords and *samurai*. The Tokugawa and their allies,
on discovering this, resorted to force, but were speed-
ily overcome. The Shogunate collapsed, the Tokugawa lands were confiscated, and the ground was
cleared for a new form of government.

Since no lord (*daimyo*) of any single clan was sufficiently powerful to wear the mantle of authority
that had been torn from the shoulders of the last
Tokugawa *Shogun*, it was draped about the Emperor
once more.[1] The ancient loyalty to the Sovereign had
never died out completely even in the darkest days
of feudalism, and the eighteenth and nineteenth centuries had seen a distinct revival of deeply emotional
reverence for the Emperor. The new leaders, having
no inherent right of their own to demand the support

---

[1] It is often said that the predominance of the Choshu and
Satsuma clans, during the Restoration and in the government
afterwards, was so great that they almost erected a new Shogunate.
The old idea that the Restoration was the product principally of
clan machinations has for some time been put aside, however,
in favor of a broader and more economic interpretation. It is
true that Lords Mori (Choshu) and Shimazu (Satsuma) were the
principal *tozama-daimyo* (outer-lords), and as such were those
from whom the Shogunate had always had most to fear. It was
only in concert with other lords, nevertheless, that they were able
to organize a new government, and at first many of the leaders
of this government were drawn from the *Kuge* (Court-Noble)
class. That the two clans were able to retain their predominance
in civil government afterwards was principally the result of their
ability to produce such outstanding personalities as Ito and
Yamagata (Choshu), and Matsukata and Okubo (Satsuma), and
thus largely control the *oligarchy*, which actually determined policy. In this study, therefore, the oligarchy, rather than these two
clans, will be emphasized.

It must also be kept in mind that Choshu early gained control
of the officer corps in the army, and Satsuma in the navy. A good
short discussion of this situation is to be found in K. W. Colegrove, *Militarism in Japan* (Boston, 1936). With particular reference
to the navy, see also Edwin Falk, *Togo and the Rise of Japanese
Sea Power* (New York, 1936).

of the people, took advantage of this love for the Emperor and did all in their power to foster it, turning it into a veritable cult of Emperor-worship.[2] They were satisfied to rule Japan from behind this façade. But who were these actual rulers of Japan to be? Who were the men who would stand behind the shelter of the throne and manipulate the strings of government?

This was the question troubling many ambitious men. In order to allay the suspicions of the *daimyo* and their *samurai* that some small group would usurp the imperial power and would rule solely in its own interests, the leaders of the restoration movement had the Emperor issue an Imperial Oath in June 1868, the first article of which read, "The practice of discussion and debate shall be universally adopted, and all measures shall be decided by public argument."[3] This was relatively noncommittal, but at least it was an acceptance of the principle that the

[2] Parallel with the interest in Dutch learning which marked the latter half of the Tokugawa period, there developed a revival of native learning which may very possibly be considered more important, and which certainly enlisted the talents of the greatest scholars of the period. Such works as the "Commentary on the Records of Ancient Matters" (*Kojiki-den*) of Motoori Norinaga; the "History of Great Japan" (*Dai Nihonshi*) produced under the auspices of the Mito branch of the Tokugawa family; and the "Unofficial History of Japan" (*Nihon Gaishi*) of Rai Jo—all contributed materially to a growing sense of the divine descent and righteous majesty of the Imperial line and of the illegitimacy of the Tokugawa "usurpation." This was coupled with a revival of "pure Shinto," which at once attempted to purge Shinto of the Buddhist elements that had been so large a part of it for a thousand years, and injected into it a cult of Emperor deification more concentrated than it had ever been before. Under the Meiji Emperor, after the Restoration, this was so intensified as to lead some Western scholars to remark that it was an entirely new aspect of Japanese thought.

[3] W. W. McLaren, "Japanese Government Documents," *Transactions of The Asiatic Society of Japan*, Vol. XLII, Part 1 (Tokyo, May 1914), p. 8.

people—meaning the *samurai* class—should have a voice in the matter of how they were to be ruled. However, this Imperial Oath in time came to be interpreted by the exponents of representative government, as follows: "An Assembly widely convoked shall be established, and thus great stress shall be laid upon public opinion."[4] This was to plague the lives of the new rulers who probably had no intention at first of establishing any such national assembly, but who now found themselves open to the accusation of disobeying the command of the Emperor, and were thus forced eventually to grant an Imperial Diet to the people in the Constitution of 1889.

During the first few years of the new regime, however, one temporary administration was set up after another with bewildering rapidity. All were characterized by the nominal leadership of Imperial Princes, Court Nobles, and great feudal *daimyo*, while the real leadership, which was largely concentrated in the hands of *samurai* from the four great western clans, operated behind this façade of great names in the offices of advisors and councillors. As well, a pretense of consulting public opinion was always maintained by the establishment of some sort of national assembly to which delegates were sent by the various feudal fiefs, and later, after these were abolished, by the prefectures. These assemblies, however, never had any actual power. They were simply glorified debating societies, with even the topics for discussion strictly limited to relatively inconsequential matters.

THE ABOLITION OF FEUDALISM

In 1868 an official of the government was placed in each fief to take charge of relations between it

[4] *Ibid.*

and the central authorities, and regulations were promulgated making all these local administrations uniform. The following year, Lords Shimazu of Satsuma, Mori of Choshu, Nabeshima of Hizen, and Yamanouchi of Tosa loyally returned their feudal domains to the Emperor, who then graciously requested all the other *daimyo* to follow suit. This move of the four great lords of western Japan was undoubtedly startling to the other feudal barons, but it was quite understandable. These men were relinquishing power and wealth only in the anticipation of acquiring even more in return. At least such was the line of argument put before them by their enterprising and ambitious *samurai* who were the real leaders of this regime, and in whose competent hands these lords were virtually helpless. In 1870 Lords Shimazu of Satsuma, Mori of Choshu, and Yamanouchi of Tosa agreed to move permanently to the new capital, Tokyo (old Edo), and to place their feudal troops at the command of the central authorities. High positions in the government were found for Itagaki Taisuke of Tosa, Saigo Takamori of Satsuma, and Okuma Shigenobu of Hizen. The Court Noble Iwakura Tomoyoshi made sure of the support of the Tokugawa clan of Owari and a very important hereditary vassal of the Tokugawa, the Lord of Hikone. Thereupon, in August 1871 an Imperial Rescript was promulgated abolishing the feudal fiefs and clans and putting an end to feudalism.

All this was quite disturbing to the *daimyo* and their *samurai* but there were none who dared oppose the will of the four great western clans of Satsuma, Choshu, Tosa, and Hizen. The *daimyo* were well paid, moreover, to acquiesce in the abolition of the feudal order. They received an annual pension of one-tenth the nominal income derived from their former estates. Since the nominal income was considerably higher than the actual income, since the *daimyo* was relieved of the responsibility of caring for his *samurai* and his many feudal servants, and since most of his debts were canceled or shouldered by the new imperial government, he was actually better off financially than he had been under the old order. Some won important positions in the government, and a large majority received patents of nobility in a new hierarchy in which no distinction was made between Court Nobles (*Kuge*) and Feudal Barons (*Buke*).

Ordinary *samurai* did not fare so well. Their nominal and actual incomes were the same; and small as they already were, the fifty per cent reduction provided for in the original plan of 1871 brought great hardship for many. They were also deeply outraged by the promulgation of a conscription law that opened the fighting services to all able-bodied men in Japan. Consequently there were undercurrents of discontent, but the *samurai* were too bewildered by all these sudden changes to know what to do. Among them, moreover, there were many more enterprising individuals who were fast being placed in the new scheme of things. While the economic position of the *samurai* was endangered by the abolition of feudalism, permission was given them at the same time to lay aside their two swords and enter upon whatever kind of commercial or financial activity they might desire. Thus, from these lower class *samurai* there emerged many individuals who, rather than the old townsmen class (*chonin*), laid the foundation for the present structure of Japanese capitalist enterprise.

The wealthy merchants, rice dealers, and money changers of Osaka, such as the Mitsui and Sumitomo families, who had financed the Imperial Restoration movement, arranged that the new regime assume the debts owed them and received various government contracts; they, therefore, were delighted with the overthrow of the old order. A large group of the bourgeoisie held mortgages on farm lands because of debts owed them by the clans and the farmers. Under feudalism farmers were not permitted to alienate their land, so that these mortgages were extralegal. The new regime now honored them and converted them into ownership rights, making these fortunate bourgeois absentee landlords, and the farmers their tenants. Moreover, the townspeople were now permitted to engage in any profession they chose to pursue, and to enter politics if they so desired. Consequently, the bourgeoisie were glad to see feudalism destroyed.

The economic status of the ordinary farmer, representing perhaps eighty per cent of the population, remained virtually unchanged.[5] However, he now had the right to go wherever he wished, and the privilege to bear arms. The former right made the growth of a laboring class possible, and the latter privilege may yet prove to be the most fundamental and far-

[5] As the system of census taking in Japan was unreliable until 1920, it is impossible to approach exactness in absolute or percentage figures for population in this early period. Estimates of the proportion of farmers to all gainfully employed workers are given in Ishii Ryoichi, *Population Pressure and Economic Life in Japan* (London, 1937), pp. 77-81, and of the distribution of rural and urban population in A. E. Hindmarsh, *The Basis of Japanese Foreign Policy* (Cambridge, 1936), pp. 56-57. These estimates, based on generalized and approximate figures, indicate that at the time of the abolition of feudalism, the proportion of the total population which depended upon agriculture for its livelihood was probably not more than ninety per cent and not less than seventy-seven per cent.

reaching change in Japanese society since the farmers were disarmed as a class at the close of the sixteenth century.

All these pensions paid the *daimyo* and their *samurai* placed an annual burden of twenty million *yen* on the new government. This was more than it could pay so long as it was forbidden by the so-called "unequal treaties," virtually forced upon the tottering Shogunate by foreign powers, to raise the tariff. Consequently, in 1871 an embassy headed by Iwakura Tomoyoshi(K)[6] and including Kido Koin(C),

[6] To show the reader that almost all the important officials of this period were appointed from among the *samurai* of one of the four great western clans, the Court Nobility (*Kuge*), or the ex-officials of the Shogunate (*Bakufu*), the following letters are used in the text:

  (B) *Bakufu,* former officials or sons of officials of the Tokugawa Shogunate
  (K) *Kuge,* Court Nobles
  (S) *samurai* from Satsuma
  (C) *samurai* from Choshu
  (H) *samurai* from Hizen
  (T) *samurai* from Tosa

Forty-three men in all held the key positions of Prime Minister (*Dajodaijin*), Great Minister of the Left (*Sadaijin*), Great Minister of the Right (*Udaijin*), Imperial Adviser (*Sangi*), and Minister (*Daijin*) of a ministry (*sho*) during the twenty years from 1869 to 1889. These were **Prime Minister:** (1871-1885) Sanjo Saneyoshi(K); **Great Minister of the Left:** (1874-1875) Shimazu Hisamitsu (*Daimyo* of Satsuma), and Taruhito-Shinno (an Imperial Prince); **Great Minister of the Right:** (1869-1871) Sanjo Saneyoshi(K), and (1871-1883) Iwakura Tomoyoshi(K); **Imperial Advisors:** Okubo Toshimichi, Saigo Takamori, Terajima Munenori, Ijichi Masaharu, Kuroda Kiyotaka, Saigo Tsugumichi, and Kawamura Sumiyoshi of Satsuma; Maebara Issei, Hirosawa Saneomi, Kido Koin, Ito Hirobumi, Yamagata Aritomo, Yamada Akiyoshi, and Inoue Kaoru—of Choshu; Itagaki Taisuke, Goto Shojiro, Sasaki Takayuki, and Fukuoka Kotei—of Tosa; Soejima Taneomi, Okuma Shigenobu, Oki Takato, and Eto Shimpei—of Hizen; and Katsu Yasuyoshi (or Awa), the former head admiral of the Shogunate's fleet. **Ministers of administrative departments** were: Date Muneki (*Daimyo* of Iyo), Enomoto Buyo(B), Hijikata Hisamoto(T), Kono Togama(T), Matsudaira Yoshinaga (Tokugawa *Daimyo* of Echizen), Matsukata Masayoshi(S), Mori Arinori(S), Oyama Iwao(S), Sano Tsune-

Ito Hirobumi(C), and Okubo Toshimichi(S), was dispatched to Europe and America to effect a revision of these treaties. The mission failed and these important leaders had to hasten back to Japan in 1873 to prevent a political storm from wrecking the new regime.

Korea was maintaining a diplomatic policy of haughty aloofness that enraged a large part of the new element in Japan that had turned towards the outside world the interest and energy that fate no longer permitted them to concentrate exclusively on their country's internal affairs. Formosan aborigines, moreover, had killed several castaways from the Japanese-controlled Ryu Kyu Islands; and the Chinese government, which claimed suzerainty over Formosa, showed no sign of meting out appropriate punishment to the offenders. A strong group in the government was clamoring for war.

By September 1873 the envoys were all back in Japan. Having visited the West, and having been influenced profoundly by what they had seen, these men felt that Japan should set her own house in order before pursuing a dangerous foreign policy. They realized how weak their country was economi-

---

tami(H), Sawa Nobuyoshi(K), Tanaka Fujimaro (samurai of Tokugawa fief of Owari), Tani Kanjo(T), Yamao Yozo(C), Yoshikawa Kensei of Awa in Shikoku, one Imperial Prince, and one more Court Noble(K).

Many who served as Imperial Advisers also held posts as Ministers from time to time. This list leaves no doubt as to who were the real leaders in the restoration movement and what class of society they represented. There were but some two hundred and eighty-six daimyo families, some one hundred and fifty families of court nobles (kuge), and some three hundred thousand samurai families, making a total of about two million people out of a population of approximately thirty-one million. Hence the leaders were drawn from a small group in an upper class that constituted only seven per cent of the population. These figures are, of course, generalized, but that cannot affect the conclusion.

cally as well as politically and how much had to be done internally to safeguard her independence. Consequently Kido(C), Iwakura(K), Okubo(S), and Ito(C) all voted for peace, and as the prestige of these men was tremendous, they carried the day. As a result, however, the coalition government of the *samurai* from the four great western clans was split in two, and the leaders of the war party, including Soejima Taneomi(H), Saigo Takamori(S), Itagaki Taisuke(T), Eto Shimpei(H), and Goto Shojiro(T), withdrew in protest from the administration.

The peace party made haste to inaugurate a series of reforms that was to transform feudal Japan into a strongly centralized, modern state. A ministry of Home Affairs was established with Okubo Toshimichi(S) in charge, and placed in direct control over all the prefectural and city governments. At the time of the "abolition of feudalism" in 1871, when the *daimyo* had voluntarily given up their hereditary fiefs to the Emperor, they were immediately returned to their provinces in the capacity of governors (*chiji*). The inefficiency of this system was soon apparent and by this reform the *daimyo*-governor system was done away with completely.

THE STRUGGLE FOR REPRESENTATIVE INSTITUTIONS

The opponents of the government soon struck back. In January 1874 Tosa *samurai* tried to assassinate Iwakura Tomoyoshi(K). Four ex-Imperial Advisers (*Sangi*)—Eto Shimpei(H), Soejima Taneomi(H), Goto Shojiro(T), and Itagaki Taisuke(T) —launched a campaign for a national elective assembly. They knew that the majority of *samurai* were more eager to fight Koreans and Formosans than to engage in domestic reforms and therefore demanded that the oligarchy consult the will of the people as expressed through a body of duly elected representatives. The government refused; and in February, Eto Shimpei(H) resorted to direct action and headed a rebellion. Another rebellion broke out under Maebara Issei(C) in Choshu. Both uprisings were crushed and the leaders killed. The situation, however, was serious. The government decreed the creation of an Assembly of Local Governors (*Chi-hokankaigi*), promising that it might convene the following year, and in May it dispatched a small punitive expedition to Formosa under Saigo Yori-michi(S), younger brother of Saigo Takamori(S). Iwasaki, a *samurai* of Tosa, being in possession of the only Japanese-owned ocean-going vessels at this time, reaped a tremendous profit from transporting troops to Formosa, and laid the foundations for the future Mitsubishi Company, the second largest and wealthiest concern in Japan. These compromise moves so angered Kido Koin(C) that he withdrew from the government. He died in 1877.

When the Assembly of Local Governors proved on its first meeting in 1875 to be but another gathering of government-picked officials completely subservient to the ruling clique, the "outs" became vehement in their criticisms of the rulers. Thereupon a Newspaper Press Law was promulgated that threatened jail sentences and fines for all critics of the government, and the control of the Minister of Home Affairs over the local authorities was extended. This drove the opposition underground for the time being.

By August 1876 the government felt strong enough to have Minister of Finance Okuma Shigenobu revise the whole system of payments to the *daimyo* and *samurai*, which was proving too great a financial burden. Lump sums were computed on the basis of the annual pension payments previously decreed for the various classes, half of which was paid in cash and half in bonds. The total sums and the interest rates for the bonds were both arranged on a sliding scale proportionate to the annual and long-term value of the different grades of original pension payments.[7] As before, when the pension system was first established on the abolition of feudalism, the *daimyo* came off relatively well, whereas the *samurai* suffered another large cut in their incomes. It was these grants of government bonds that established the foundation of a new capitalist class in Japan, for many of the *daimyo* and their *samurai* established banks on the basis of these bonds, or invested their capital in new business enterprises that were frequently subsidized by a government which was being run by their fellow lords and *samurai*.

By this time, however, the *samurai* of Satsuma saw more clearly the true color of this "restoration" they had done so much to effect. Outraged at the law of universal conscription passed in 1873 and the increasing importance of capitalist factions, both seeming inevitably to cause the disintegration of their class, and disgusted with a foreign policy which ignored their deep interest in establishing a Japanese sphere of influence outside of Japan, they rose in desperate rebellion under the inspiring leadership of Saigo Takamori(S). Tragically, the new conscription troops, who were but despised farmers' sons, proved more than a match for the flower of feudal Japan, and although at bitter cost to themselves, they annihilated the rebel forces. Saigo Takamori committed

[7] The pension system (*Horoku*) is discussed in Honjo, *op. cit.*, see especially pp. 127, 137.

suicide and with him the proud feudal order was buried. This was the last rebellion against the new regime.

This did not mean that the government's opponents had given up direct action, for in May 1878 Home Minister Okubo Toshimichi(S) was assassinated. The authorities promptly declared their intention to establish prefectural assemblies, which they did in July. The main function of these local assemblies (*Fuken-kai*) was to discuss the prefectural budgets and new ways of raising local taxes. The Governor of the prefecture initiated all bills and had complete veto powers, under the discretion of the Home Ministry to which he was in the first instance responsible. He could suspend the meetings of the assembly, and the Home Minister could dissolve the assembly. The members were elected for a term of four years and had to pay ten *yen* per year in direct land taxes to be eligible for office. The electorate consisted of all males twenty-five years of age or over who paid five *yen* or more in annual land taxes.

The establishment of assemblies was a step, although a timid one, in the direction of representative government and it encouraged the critics of the new regime to increase their demand for a national deliberative assembly. Itagaki(T) was the leader in this movement. Although the government refused to countenance such a proposal, it granted assemblies to cities, towns, and villages in 1880 and in that year permitted the prefectural assemblies to elect standing committees from among their members to serve as advisory councils to the Governors.

It was not until 1881 that the series of events took place which made possible the Constitution of 1889. Although the *samurai* of Satsuma, Choshu, Tosa, and

Hizen had all taken part in the restoration movement, the former two, being considerably more powerful than the latter two, had received most of the important positions in the new regime. Satsuma had a virtual monopoly of the navy positions and Choshu of the army. Itagaki, the leader of the Tosa faction, was no longer in the government, while Okuma, the most important of the Hizen *samurai*, although he had been Minister of Finance for several years and was still an Imperial Adviser, was little consulted by the Satsuma and Choshu leaders. In 1881 Kuroda Kiyotaka(S), head of the Hokkaido Colonization Commission, recommended that the government sell to the members of the Commission, who had formed a private company, for a fraction of one million *yen* all the equipment and property in that island that had been bought by the Commission over a period of ten years for ten million *yen* of government money. This was barefaced graft on a large scale, and Okuma, bidding for popular support, called a meeting of the citizens of Tokyo at which he disclosed this malversation. Mobs promptly went out and burned police boxes, destroyed government property; a grave crisis threatened. Within twenty-four hours the government clique had the Emperor issue a rescript promising the creation of a national parliament in 1890. The oligarchy was so angry at Okuma, however, that he was driven out of the government and politically ruined for the time being. Itagaki(T) and Goto(T) promptly established the Liberal Party (*Jiyuto*), which was the forerunner of the present *Seiyukai*.

While the exposure of such graft did assist the advance toward representative government, it must by no means be supposed that it altogether cleansed the old politics. In this case, the government did not sell the Hokkaido property to the private company; but Kuroda(S) not only escaped disgrace but was raised to an even higher position. Even such men as Kido (C), Ito(C), Okubo(S), Itagaki(T), and Goto(T) died millionaires although they all started as poor *samurai*. Men of lesser political and moral stature frequently approached the closer to real corruption as they were less concerned for their nation's welfare.

The following year, 1882, Okuma established the Progressive Party, or *Kaishinto*—forerunner of the present *Minseito*—while Ito(C) went to America and Europe to study Western constitutions and administrative practice. He was quite impressed by Bismarck and the Prussian constitution, and returned the next year convinced that some such form of autocratic government was desirable for Japan.

Meanwhile the oligarchy had been increasing the pressure on the opposition by enforcing the press laws more and more stringently until all the large newspapers were constrained to hire so-called "jail editors" whose sole function was to serve out sentences in jail for information the papers had published. In 1884 riots due to depreciation of the paper currency occurred, but the government blamed them on the machinations of Itagaki's *Jiyuto* and had that party suppressed. At that same time Okuma found it expedient to withdraw from the *Kaishinto*.

The following year several changes in the government were made by Ito, who was preparing for the new constitution. A Cabinet was established in 1885 whose ministers were declared to be directly responsible to the Emperor alone. The Premier was a German Chancellor as regards his powers. Great stress was laid by the oligarchy on the contention that by these changes true personal rule by the Emperor had at last been achieved, in order to discourage any popular attack on the regime. A Lord Keeper of the Privy Seal (*Naidaijin*) was appointed for the first time and a civil service was inaugurated. This was intended to develop an efficient bureaucracy, but it was in fact at last to break the monopoly of offices held by the *samurai* of the four great western clans. In 1887 the Supreme War Council (*Gunji-sangi-in*) was established to advise the Emperor on matters affecting the fighting forces. That same year the government took another step toward crushing all opposition by promulgating a Peace Preservation Ordinance virtually declaring martial law in Tokyo. Secret societies and assemblies were forbidden. People who disturbed the peace were subject to imprisonment. All persons living within seven and one-half miles of the Imperial Palace who were considered troublemakers by the authorities were ordered to leave that area within twenty-four hours. This drove most of the antiadministration leaders out of the capital.

In 1888 the Privy Council (*Sumitsu-in*) was created with Ito Hirobumi as President, to discuss the constitution that Ito had been writing.

Finally, on February 11, 1889, the 2,549th anniversary of the founding of the Japanese Empire by its first sovereign, the new constitution was promulgated. All the radical newspapers had been suppressed and the others were forbidden to comment on the document. The constitution had been drawn up in secret, and it was read to an audience of select officials from which the general public was excluded. The Imperial Speech on the promulgation of the constitution began with these words: "Whereas We make it the joy and glory of Our heart to behold the prosperity of Our country, and the welfare of Our subjects, We do hereby, in virtue of the supreme power We inherit from Our Imperial Ancestors, promulgate the present immutable fundamental law, for the sake of Our present subjects and their descendants." The opening sentences of the Preamble to the Constitution contained the following, "Having, by virtue of the glories of Our Ancestors, ascended the Throne in lineal succession unbroken for ages eternal—," and "The rights of sovereignty of the State, We have inherited from Our Ancestors, and We shall bequeath them to Our descendants. Neither We nor they shall in future fail to wield them, in accordance with the provisions of the Constitution hereby granted."[8]

This Constitution was quite obviously a gift of the Emperor to his people; not something they had deserved or won, but something that had been granted them through his bounteous mercy.[9] Not even a pretence was made that this was to be a government of, for, or by the people. The Constitution was promulgated in a spirit of autocracy and has been interpreted in such a spirit with but slight and temporary changes ever since.

[8] McLaren, "Japanese Government Documents," cited, pp. 133-134.

[9] In the period of party government, during the decade following the World War, liberalism waxed strong enough actually to make possible a controversy on the question, Was the Constitution the Emperor's gift, or the nation's right? When one school of thought, however, went so far as to claim that the Emperor was but an organ and not the essence of the State, the general reaction was almost hysterical. Since the return to a more singly defined attitude towards Japanese institutions and destinies after 1932, the old idea that the Constitution is the Emperor's gift to his people again prevails. For a careful discussion of this subject, see Takeuchi Tatsuji, *War and Diplomacy in the Japanese Empire* (New York, 1935), Ch. I, II.

CHAPTER IV

THE PRESENT ORGANIZATION OF THE JAPANESE GOVERNMENT

IT IS only after one has grasped the fundamentals of Japanese political theory, namely, that society is more important than the individual, that all men are by nature unequal, that politics is synonymous with ethics, that government by man is superior to government by law, and that the patriarchal family is the ideal state; and only after one has studied the evolution of the Japanese government through the successive stages of a primitive tribal theocracy, a bureaucratic civil aristocracy, and a military aristocracy which in its later years was losing its power to the rising bourgeoisie—that one is able to understand the Constitution of 1889 and the subsequent history of so-called "constitutional government" in Japan. Without this background one is in grave danger of interpreting Japanese political institutions from the point of view of Western liberal democracy. It is true that European political theories and Occidental forms of government exerted a great deal of influence on the minds of leading Japanese statesmen and thus played a part in shaping the organization and policy of the new regime. Nevertheless, the vast majority of officials and the common people have never studied Western political institutions, nor have they been influenced in any marked degree by European and American political doctrines. Being well acquainted only with their own history, they cannot help but look upon their present form of government as a logical twentieth-century evolution from more ancient forms.

Approaching the problem from this point of view, it then becomes fairly evident that the new form of government established by the Constitution of 1889 almost inevitably had to center about a theocratic sovereign who was to delegate his powers to an aristocracy. This aristocracy had to be rather definitely divided into a civil and a military oligarchy that would function with almost complete independence of each other, as such dual government had been customary in Japan since the close of the twelfth century. It is also evident that this government had to make a new place in politics for the rising bourgeoisie, and that the leaders of this new middle class would look for guidance to those countries of the West where their social equals had already won control of the state; and would attempt to duplicate in Japan those middle-class political institutions that would bring them the power they desired.

Consequently, one must not study the Japanese government as a Western constitutional regime transplanted to the Far East, but as an oriental plant that has been placed in an occidental flowerpot, been watered with Western liberalism and fertilized with European and American political doctrines, but which still bears Japanese flowers and fruit, although these are now somewhat peculiarly and disturbingly different from anything the plant has borne before. Thus Baron Hozumi, an eminent jurist and former president of the Privy Council, in trying to explain just what the Japanese government has become, wrote that "The Emperor holds the sovereign power, not as his own inherent right, but as an inheritance

from his Divine Ancestor. The government is, therefore, theocratical. The Emperor rules over the country as the supreme head of the vast family of the
Japanese nation. The government is, therefore, patriarchal. The Emperor exercises the sovereign power
according to the Constitution, which is based on the
most advanced principles of modern constitutional-
ism. The government is, therefore, constitutional. In
other words, the fundamental principle of the Japanese government is theocratic-patriarchal constitu-
tionalism."[1]

Since the Japanese government is so different from
those of the West, it is unwise to describe it in terms
of the familiar categories of the executive, legislature,
and the judiciary, since no real attempt was made to
differentiate among these organs of the government.
Moreover, since Japanese politics is primarily concerned with men rather than with political institutions, the study of the latter should be subordinated
to that of the former. Consequently, the Japanese
government is most easily understood when described in terms of the law, the aristocrats, the bureaucrats, the militarists, the politicians, and the
people, for the present regime has been built not primarily around theories and institutions, but around
men and the special classes of society they represent.
The Cabinet is the battlefield where these groups
struggle, and the citadel of power that each tries to
conquer.

THE LAW

The law of the Japanese Empire may be roughly
divided into the Japanese Constitution, the Imperial
House Law, imperial ordinances, statutes, and
treaties.

[1] In Baron Hozumi, *Ancestor Worship and Japanese Law*
(Tokyo, 1901), pp. 87-88.

The very existence of a written constitution was unmistakable proof of the influence of Western political thought on the governing class of Japan. It meant at least a superficial change from government by man to government by law; but the framers of the document took care to preserve almost intact the political privileges of the ruling oligarchy. In order to do this, they made the institution of monarchy unassailable and then operated from behind this bulwark.

1. *The Constitution*

The Constitution of 1889 is declared to be a gift of the Emperor to his people. Consequently, only he can initiate any amendment. Such amendments have to be approved by the House of Peers (*Kizoku-in*) and the House of Representatives (*Shugi-in*) to be effective. The people can, therefore, at least prevent a change in the constitution. Thus, the constitution is rigid, and no amendment has yet been made. The interpretation of this document is left to the organs of government concerned, which means primarily the judges of the courts. Only when there is a conflict of opinion between different organs of the government is the matter settled by the Privy Council, which is therefore called the "watchdog of the constitution." Finally, the constitution is above all ordinary law, and the Imperial House Law, while not superior to the constitution, stands apart from it.[2]

2. *The Imperial House Law*

The Imperial House Law is second in importance only to the constitution itself, and was promulgated at the same time. It is superior to all ordinary legislation and cannot be supplanted or amended by such.

[2] A translation of the Constitution appears as an appendix in Takeuchi, *op. cit.*

Consequently, it is completely outside the control of the Imperial Diet. It can be amended only "by the Emperor, with the advice of the Imperial Family Council and with that of the Privy Council."[3] Article II of the constitution reads, "The Imperial Throne shall be succeeded to by Imperial male descendants, according to the provisions of the Imperial House Law," and Article XVII states in part that, "A Regency shall be instituted in conformity with the provisions of the Imperial House Law." It is quite clear, then, that the whole problem of who shall be the Emperor is not settled by the constitution, but by the laws governing the Imperial Family.

3. *Imperial Ordinances*

The ordinance powers of the Emperor are very great. Imperial ordinances are of three types: prerogative, administrative, and emergency ordinances. The first includes such ordinances as the Imperial House Law, the Peerage Ordinances, etc., while the second includes executive ordinances issued to preserve the general welfare. The Diet has no control over such ordinances. The most important ordinances fall in the third category. They may be issued to deal with emergencies while the Diet is not in session, and when it cannot be called in time to consider the situation. The scope of such ordinances is unlimited, but they must be approved by the Privy Council (*Sumitsu-in*) before being promulgated, and must be accepted by the Diet at its next session, if they are to remain in effect. Should the Diet withhold its approval, however, such a decision can have no retro-

[3] Article LXII of the Imperial House Law. A translation of the Imperial House Law may be found as an appendix to H. S. Quigley, *Japanese Government and Politics* (New York, 1932).

active effects. Moreover, should the government repeal a new ordinance prior to the next session of the Diet, it is not obligated to place the matter before the Diet, and may even refuse to allow it to be discussed should that prove embarrassing to the administration. All imperial ordinances to be valid must bear the countersignature of some minister of state, for the Emperor never acts except on the advice of some high official who must bear responsibility for the act. These officials, however, are responsible only to the Emperor.

4. *Statutes*

Statutes require a majority vote of each House. The legislative power of the House of Peers (*Kizoku-in*) is equal to that of the House of Representatives (*Shugi-in*) with the sole exception that financial bills must be initiated in the Lower House. The Upper House alone, however, enjoys the privileges of freedom from dissolution, settlement of disputed elections of its own members, amendment of the ordinance concerning its own organization, and consultation by the Emperor upon matters affecting the Nobility as a class. The Emperor has absolute veto power over all laws. If some exercise of this power might raise a popular furor, the government can simply delay publishing the act in the Official Gazette, which publication brings the said act into effect, or it may fail to provide in the budget for necessary funds to enforce the act. Consequently, there is no danger that the Diet will pass a law that is unacceptable to the administration. Customary Diet procedure, moreover, follows a European rather than an American model, for bills are ordinarily presented to the Diet by the Government, and not by a representative from the floor.

5. *International Treaties and Agreements*

Treaties are ratified by the Emperor; Article XIII of the Constitution states that, "The Emperor declares war, makes peace and concludes treaties." The Diet has no control over such international commitments, although the administration must obtain the consent of the Privy Council (*Sumitsu-in*) before the Emperor signs the treaty. Even when the treaty creates additional expenditures, such payments are considered to be fixed expenditures, which, under Article LXVII of the Constitution, are not subject to change by the Imperial Diet. At least to date the Diet has never failed to pass the necessary financial legislation to make the enforcement of such treaties possible. Treaties cannot be altered by ordinances or statutes, and hence are superior to ordinary law, but they must not conflict with the Constitution or the Imperial House Law.[4]

THE ARISTOCRATS

The Imperial Family, the Elder Statesmen (*Genro*), and the House of Peers (*Kizoku-in*) constitute the aristocratic element in the Japanese government. All the old families of the Court Nobles (*Kuge*), the Feudal Barons (*Buke*), and the lords (*daimyo*), the *samurai* who played important roles in the Imperial Restoration, and the wealthy bourgeoisie who received patents of nobility for their financial assistance to the new regime, and finally

[4] This subject has not been so well defined in practice as it may seem in theory. For a penetrating discussion see Takeuchi, *op. cit.*, which discusses Japanese Government with primary reference to this whole problem.

the cream of the professional class, belong to this group.

1. *The Emperor*

Article IV of the Constitution declares that, "The Emperor is the head of the Empire, combining in Himself the rights of sovereignty, and exercises them, according to the provisions of the present constitution." He has the right to convoke, open, close, and prorogue the Imperial Diet and to dissolve the House of Representatives. He issues ordinances and determines the organization of the various branches of the administration, the salaries, appointments and dismissals of all civil and military officials, except when otherwise provided for in the constitution. He is at once generalissimo of the field army and navy, and supreme commander over military and naval administration. He declares war, makes peace, and concludes treaties, declares a state of martial law, confers titles of nobility and other honors, proclaims amnesties, and issues pardons or commutations of sentences. The judicature is "exercised by courts of law, according to law, in the name of the Emperor." His power to appoint and remove judges is unlimited.

In other words, the Emperor's prerogatives are so numerous and extensive that few, if any, attributes of sovereignty are omitted from the list. The important fact to remember, however, is not so much that the Emperor is virtually the State, as that the Emperor never acts except on the advice of others. Under the present system of Japanese government, Imperial decrees, ordinances, and orders are issued over the countersignatures of the ministers of the administrative departments affected; and with reference to Imperial Household affairs, the Imperial

Household Minister has similar responsibilities. The Emperor is not expected to manifest a will of his own, except insofar as he may persuade his advisors to alter whatever advice they had originally contemplated.

To find the real rulers of Japan one must search beyond the Emperor. Perhaps the word "shield" would be the best description of the role played by the Sovereign; for the long tradition of the Imperial Family, and the burning loyalty of the common people to this symbol of national unity, make the Emperor a perfect shield against a public irate and ready to hurl imprecations at its ruling officials. No one criticizes the Throne. Yet such a policy of hiding behind the Emperor cannot be pursued too far. It has broken down several times before in the course of Japanese history, for violent reaction may always have recourse at least to the forcible replacement of the imperial advisors.

2. *The Imperial Family Council*

The Emperor's prerogative over Imperial Household affairs is based on the fact that he is the patriarch of the Imperial Family. He conducts family affairs, in accordance with the provisions laid down in the Imperial House Law and with the advice of the Imperial Family Council. This body is composed of all Princes of the Blood who have reached their majority.

The Imperial Family receives a yearly appropriation from the Diet of 4,500,000 *yen* (1,500,000 dollars) for the expenses of the court. In addition it obtains a substantial income from its agricultural and forest lands, and its blocks of shares in various banks and commercial companies. The value of its holdings is estimated at over one billion *yen* (330,-000,000 dollars), making it almost the wealthiest family in Japan. The Imperial Family Council has a considerable voice in the control and spending of this vast fortune.

3. *The Genro, or Elder Statesmen*

Undoubtedly the best-known feature of Japanese government among Westerners is that group of men known as the *Genro*, or Elder Statesmen. They are not mentioned in the constitution, nor are there any provisions in the ordinary laws and ordinances regarding the legal status of such a body. However, these Elder Statesmen have exercised more political power than any other persons in Japan.

Although it cannot be said exactly when this group of all-important advisers to the Emperor came into existence, and although one cannot state with absolute certainty just who belonged to it and who did not, nevertheless such a body did make its presence felt in public life a little before 1900. This does not mean that such a group did not exist prior to that time; but it was only after the Constitution of 1889 had brought some sort of order and permanency to the political structure, and various organs of government had started to crystallize into recognizable and definable forms, that the public began to realize that an extraconstitutional body of experienced and trusted statesmen met privately and settled momentous affairs of state behind the façade of the new regime. The members of this group were thereupon called the Elder Statesmen.[5]

[5] It is a common fallacy among Western observers to think of the *Genro* in the same terms as they think of the modern Japanese government. It should be understood that by the term *Genro*, a specific man or specific men are meant. For this reason, special

It is these men who have been the real power behind the Throne. It became customary for their opinion to be asked and, more important still, to be followed in all matters of great significance to the welfare of the state. No Premier was ever appointed except on the recommendation of these men who became known as *Genro*. Until 1922 no important domestic legislation, no important foreign treaty escaped their perusal and sanction before it was signed by the Emperor. These men, in their time, were the actual rulers of Japan.

The original group was composed of Ito Hirobumi, Yamagata Aritomo, and Inoue Kaoru of the Choshu clan, and Oyama Iwao and Matsukata Masayoshi of the Satsuma clan—all men who had played stellar roles in the political history of the Meiji Restoration. They were defendants of so-called "clan" or autocratic government against the advance of democratic, representative institutions. Later additions to the group were Katsura Taro(C), and Saionji Kimmochi, the only Court Noble (*Kuge*) among the *Genro* and the only living member today, as Ito was assassinated in 1909, Katsura died in 1913, Inoue in 1915, Oyama in 1916, Yamagata in 1922, and Matsukata in 1924.

4. *The House of Peers*

The House of Peers (*Kizoku-in*) consists of: all the Princes of the Blood—at present 18 in number—

emphasis may be justified on the fact that these Elder Statesmen were, no less than their contemporaries, considered politicians until well toward the close of the nineteenth century. The existence of the *Genro* as a respected council with powers and prerogatives based on an unwritten but very real law was a phenomenon that appeared only late in the modernization of Japan, and that will disappear as such with the death of the aged Prince Saionji, who is approaching his ninetieth year.

who are of age; all princes and marquises over twenty-nine years of age—at present about 49 in number; 18 counts, 66 viscounts, and 66 barons elected from among their respective orders for seven-year terms; never more than 125 imperial appointees for life, chosen for special service to the state or for distinguished scholarship; 4 members of the Imperial Academy elected for a seven-year term by their associates; and finally, a group elected by and from the highest taxpayers of each prefecture, a group numbering at present about 66 persons.

Naturally such a conglomeration tends to be highly conservative, and since its legislative powers equal those of the House of Representatives, it has proved a bulwark of autocracy. Peers can and do serve as premiers and cabinet ministers. Prince Konoe, the present premier, was President of the House of Peers from 1933 until he assumed the premiership in 1937. Parties in the House of Peers differ from those in the House of Representatives; the Peers are opposed to popular party cabinets and abhor co-operation with party politicians. Although there is always much talk among liberals about the need for reform in the House of Peers, no such step can be taken without the consent of the Peers themselves, consequently no fundamental change has ever been made.

It is not difficult to see how the aristocracy, operating through the Imperial Family Council, the Elder Statesmen, and the House of Peers, was guaranteed a virtually unassailable position in the government by the Constitution of 1889.

THE BUREAUCRATS

A second group in the Japanese government consists of the bureaucrats, men who hold civil posts not because of their birth or wealth, but because of their political abilities. They are government appointees, not elected officials. Their loyalty is to the ruling class of which they consider themselves a very important part, not to the common people whom they consider a different and inferior class. The leaders of the bureauracy are the Lord Keeper of the Privy Seal, the Minister of the Imperial Household, and the Privy Councillors, whereas the four hundred and fifty thousand or so members of the civil service constitute its rank and file.

1. *Imperial Household Ministry*

The Lord Keeper of the Privy Seal is particularly influential because of his close personal relationship with the Emperor and his possession of the Imperial and State Seals which must be attached to all Imperial ordinances and laws to make them official. He is, therefore, a very powerful adviser of the Emperor. The Minister of the Imperial Household is in charge of all matters pertaining to the Imperial Family and to the Emperor as a member of this family. Although called a Minister he is not a member of the Cabinet and is unaffected by cabinet changes. All titles of nobility and rank conferred by the Emperor are done with the advice of this Minister. He is also, by the nature of his duties a powerful advisor to the Throne.

Since through these two officials, appointments to see the Emperor must be made, they can prove a troublesome barrier to their political opponents if the latter should attempt to secure an Imperial audience in order to give advice on policy that does not meet with the approval of the former two.

Appointments to these posts are made by the Emperor on the advice of the Prime Minister, and dismissals are made in the same manner, although it is generally customary to allow these officials to hold their posts permanently or until they desire to resign.

2. *The Privy Council*

The Privy Council (*Sumitsu-in*) was created in 1888 to act as the supreme advisory body to the Emperor. The immediate reason for its establishment in that particular year was to enable it to deliberate upon, and accept, the constitution drawn up by Ito(C). Today it is composed of twenty-six regular members who are appointed for life by the Emperor upon nomination by the Prime Minister after approval of the Council and in particular, the President of the Council. The cabinet ministers, who generally are thirteen in number, are *ex-officio* members of this body. They are outnumbered two to one by the permanent Councillors, who are truly venerable sages, since the average age is about seventy-three years.

The Privy Council must be consulted in such important matters pertaining to the Imperial Family as a change in the order of succession of the Throne, the establishment of a regency, or an amendment to the Imperial House Law. Its sanction must be obtained for all laws and ordinances supplementary to the constitution as well as for drafts of amendments to that document. Each organ of the government has the right to interpret the constitution, but where two such interpretations so seriously conflict as to endanger the proper functioning of the government—as in the disagreement of 1892 between the two Houses of the Diet regarding their respective budgetary powers—the Council may be called upon to render a decision. It must approve of all emergency

Imperial ordinances issued when the Diet is not in session, ordinances proclaiming a state of martial law, ordinances bearing penal provisions, and matters relating to changes in the personnel, functions, or procedure of the Privy Council. Its advice on important foreign treaties and conventions must be considered before they can be ratified by the Emperor. Finally, any matter of great significance to the state is generally submitted to the Privy Council, and is not to be settled without its consent.

It is clear, therefore, that the Privy Councillors are a power in Japanese politics. The possibilities of conflict between them and the Cabinet are innumerable. Such a situation is detrimental to the efficient functioning of the government. Opposition to the Privy Council is violent in the House of Representatives and many plans for its reform and even for its abolishment have been suggested. It is quite true that the Council cannot pass judgment on any matters except those specifically laid before it by the Emperor, who always acts in this connection on the advice of the Prime Minister. As all appointments to the Privy Council are made by the Prime Minister in the name of the Emperor it would appear rather easy for the Cabinet to break the power of the Privy Council either by packing it with friends or by refusing to lay matters before its members for their perusal. Tradition and the prestige of the Councillors, however, stand in the way of so simple a solution. No one is made a Councillor until it has been ascertained that he is acceptable to the President and a majority of the members of the Privy Council. If the Premier were to disregard this custom, or were to "advise" the Emperor to dismiss certain Councillors, or would neglect to "advise" the Emperor to lay important matters before the Privy Council, he would immediately bring down upon himself a storm of criticism from the Bureaucrats, the House of Peers, the opposition party in the House of Representatives, and the Militarists, so that it would be a very courageous man, who was sure of a tremendous amount of popular support, who would dare adopt such a line of action.[6]

The Privy Council is a bulwark of authoritarian, autocratic government. The Premier, although theoretically responsible only to the Emperor, is nevertheless compelled by his office to take into account the feelings and wishes of the majority party in the House of Representatives. Should the powers of the Privy Council be drastically limited, thereby increasing the influence of the Cabinet, and should the common people, through their representatives in the Lower House, win control of the Cabinet, the Bureaucrats and Aristocrats would find themselves face to face with the public. To many of them this would be a most distasteful experience and one which they will forego as long as possible. The *Genro* are practically a thing of the past. Some group must take their place if authoritarian, aristocratic government is to be preserved. The Privy Councillors, the Lord Keeper of the Privy Seal, and the Minister of the Imperial Household are their logical successors.

3. *The Civil Service*

The civil service contains some four hundred and fifty thousand members. These men are chosen on the

[6] Premier Hamaguchi alone of the Commoner heads of the government has had the courage and the prestige directly to defy the Privy Council, in the consideration of the London Naval Treaty of 1930. In this case, when such defiance was shown, the Privy Council retreated far enough to avoid an undisguised test of power. See Takeuchi, *op. cit.*, Ch. XXV.

basis of competitive examination or on the basis of
their academic qualifications. A continual struggle
goes on between these bureaucrats and the party politicians, since the former try to extend the civil service
and to defend its members against removal from
office for political reasons, whereas the latter are
eager to encourage the spoils system. It can safely
be said that the politicians have been breaking down
the *esprit de corps* of the bureaucracy for several
years. The Ministry of Home Affairs has become the
happy hunting ground of the party politicians, while
the Ministry of Foreign Affairs remains the citadel
of the bureaucrats. The two groups are still struggling for control of the other ministries, those of War
and the Navy excluded, but the battle has been going
against the bureaucrats, at least until the recent
crisis.

THE MILITARISTS

A third group in the Japanese government are the
militarists. These are the professional soldiers who
exercise their influence in politics through the Board
of Field Marshals and Fleet Admirals, the Supreme
War Council, the "Big Three" of the Army and the
"Big Two" of the Navy, the rank and file of the
fighting forces, and the various military and patriotic societies.

1. *The Board of Field Marshals and Fleet Admirals*

The Board of Field Marshals and Fleet Admirals
(*Gensuifu*) consists of those of sufficiently high rank
to possess one or the other of these titles. Although
the Emperor is commander-in-chief of the fighting
forces, he does not act except on the advice of the
high military officials. This body can be perpetuated

only through war, as none but Imperial Princes become Field Marshals and Fleet Admirals in peacetime. Thus, at the present moment there are only three members, all of them Imperial Princes who owe their positions to their birth rather than to their abilities or experience, so that this board is relatively insignificant today.

2. *The Supreme War Council*

The Supreme War Council (*Gunji-sangi-in*) consists of the above-mentioned Field Marshals and Fleet Admirals, the Chiefs of the General Staff and the Navy Staff, the Ministers of War and the Navy, and other important army and navy officers appointed by the Emperor. All important matters dealing with the fighting services are settled by this council whose advice the Emperor always follows. The army and navy members frequently meet separately to discuss business affecting only one of the services.

3. *Army and Navy Administration*

The "Big Three" of the army are the Chief of the General Staff, the Minister of War, and the Inspector-General of Military Education; the "Big Two" of the Navy are the Chief of the Naval Staff, and the Minister of the Navy. All but the Inspector-General have the right of direct access to the Emperor. The two Chiefs of Staff are theoretically the most influential militarists, but at present two Imperial Princes are serving as such, so that the real power lies with the other three. The Ministers of War and the Navy must be active Generals, Lieutenant-Generals, Admirals, or Vice-Admirals according to the regulations drawn up by Militarist Yamagata (C). They may be chosen by the Premier, but are appointed by the Emperor only on the nomination of the army and navy members respectively in the Supreme War Council. Since the army was afraid that a Minister of War, collaborating as he must in the cabinet with bureaucrats and party politicians, might be somewhat contaminated by civilian ideology, the whole important field of military education was withdrawn from his control and entrusted to a special Inspector-General of Military Education. He also is appointed by the Emperor on the recommendation of the army members of the Supreme War Council.

Since no Cabinet can exist without Ministers of War and the Navy, and since these men must be military men subservient to the will of the Supreme War Council, the fighting services always can and frequently do bring about the downfall of any premier who pursues policies unacceptable to them.

Although all Japanese are the loyal children of the Emperor, the fighting men are looked upon as his favorites, for they are bound to him in the additional relationship of soldiers or sailors to the commander-in-chief. The fighting services, therefore, particularly the officers, feel quite superior to the rank and file of ordinary subjects. In an Imperial Rescript to the army in 1882 it was stated that "service men should not involve themselves or interest themselves in politics," and the constitution does not permit them to vote. Since the active members of the army and the navy control all military affairs, however, and since it is impossible to divorce these from financial matters, foreign policies, and the nation's whole economic setup, the militarists are very much in politics.

Consequently, they are interested in educating the

public to think along the same channels with the leaders of the fighting services. For this reason there are all sorts of militaristic organizations and societies for everyone from simple ex-service men to the most burning patriots. Such are: the Imperial Ex-Servicemen's Association (*Teikoku-zaigo-gunjin-kai*) with a membership of three million; the notorious Black Dragon Society (*Kokuryu-kai*)[7] and the Black Ocean Society (*Gen'yosha*),[8] to mention only a few of them. Their programs are all imperialistic. They glorify war and the fighting man, lay great stress on loyalty to the Emperor, and are fascist in their economic ideology.

THE POLITICIANS

The politicians are those whose tenure of office depends upon the votes of the electorate. They are the "representatives of the common people." They are to be found in the Lower House of the Diet and in the political parties, and they have been working their way into the lower brackets of the bureaucracy through progressive extension of the spoils system.

[7] The *Kokuryu-kai* came into existence at the time of the Russo-Japanese War. It was primarily directed towards the establishment of a Japanese sphere of interest in Siberia. Despite the fact that it was much favored by ex-service men and was said to have direct contact with the army, it became notorious for its espionage and intrigue. After it came into disfavor, with the "Anglo-Saxonization" of the Japanese government, it became one of the open proponents of "direct action."

[8] The *Gen'yosha* was formed shortly after the Satsuma uprising of 1877-78, as a proponent of the maritime and continental expansion movement with which the rebelling Satsuma *samurai* were so closely identified. It concentrated on organizing the Tosa and Hizen group—Okuma, and Itagaki—into direct opposition to the Ito-Okubo Government. It has continued to press for a "positive" expansionist government policy. For an interesting discussion of these and other "secret societies," which suffers remarkably little in objectivity, although it is written by two Soviet Russians, see Tanin and Yohan, *Militarism and Fascism in Japan* (New York, 1934).

1. *The House of Representatives*

The House of Representatives (*Shugi-in*) consists of four hundred and sixty-six members chosen for a term of four years. It is convoked annually by the Emperor, meeting for a period of three months. It generally opens in late December and then promptly recesses until after the New Year's festivities, usually closing in late March. Extraordinary sessions may be called by the Emperor at any time. The Emperor has the power to prorogue the Diet as often as he wishes, but not for more than fifteen days at any single time. He can dissolve the House of Representatives at will, but a general election must be held soon after, since the new House must meet within five months of the dissolution of the old.

All statutes require passage by a majority vote of each House, and every emergency imperial ordinance must be approved by the Diet at its next session to remain in effect. Its consent is necessary before any amendment can be made to the constitution. It has the power to initiate legislation, but most bills are introduced by the administration. Its financial powers are strictly limited. It has no control over items in the budget listed as fixed expenditures, such as the salaries of officials, expenses of the Imperial Household, ordinary expenditures of the various branches of the administration, the army and navy, expenses arising from treaties, expenditures that may have arisen by the effect of law and that arise from the legal obligations of the government. Parliament has no budgetary control over administrative dues or other revenue having the nature of compensation, such as are derived from the post office, government railways, passports, and so forth. Moreover, Article LXXI states that, "When the Imperial Diet has not voted on the budget, or when the budget has not been brought into actual existence, the government shall carry out the budget of the preceding year." Consequently, the Diet does not hold the purse strings, and hence finds itself in a very weak position with reference to the administration.

2. *Political Parties*

Political parties in Japan have not revolved about principles, but about men. The two original parties, the *Jiyuto* and the *Kaishinto*, were established by Itagaki(T) and Okuma(H) respectively, because these gentlemen were angry at the way the *samurai* of Satsuma and Choshu were monopolizing all the good positions in the government. They used their parties as tools with which to pry open lucrative posts in the administration for themselves and their loyal henchmen. These parties, after passing through several metamorphoses, have now become the Seiyukai and the Minseito.

By what program they severally manage to attract their members, it would be difficult to say, unless it be the spoils system. They have been primarily groups of professional politicians who rally about the man most likely to be able to furnish them with easy positions at good salaries, or better yet, with possibilities for making lucrative financial bargains with commercial and industrial magnates. Corruption and malversation in and out of office have become so much identified with the idea "politician" in Japanese life that it has been easy for the militarist group to use as a premise for all their claims, the inherent viciousness of politicians as a class.

Whatever the several parties do offer in the way of broad programs, generally seems close to, or perhaps derived from, the basic policies of the several great capitalist organizations of Japan. It has frequently been said that these parties are nothing more than the tools of the great companies; while this may be too strong, there is no doubt that the Mitsui has associated itself primarily with the *Seiyukai*, and the Mitsubishi with the *Minseito*. As a result, elements which favor an economic system approaching more nearly what is known as fascism in the West, have not hesitated to accuse the major parties of being organized gangs bent on plundering the public domain and treasury in the interests of their masters, the capitalists. It is hoped, on the other hand, by the advocates of democratic institutions that the persecution the parties have endured at the hands of such castigators during the past few years will develop their integrity and work eventually to improve their reputation among the general public.

There have been many lesser parties centering about ambitious politicians who have quarreled with the leader of one of the two main parties, but these have been quite ephemeral organizations that generally dissolve as soon as their members have been granted some share of the spoils by one of the larger parties, or when the members have lost faith in their leaders' capacities to acquire such.

A few notable exceptions are the "mass" parties which are socialist[9] in philosophy and make their

---

[9] While popular movements, of course, had existed for some time before, it was not until after the granting of universal man-

appeal to the farmers and laborers. Although they have never been strong enough to win more than a very few offices, the members are almost fanatical in their allegiance to principles. Therefore, although weak, they command the respect of many people. The socialist movement has been hampered by the ideological quarrels among its leaders; but here again, as in the case of the political parties, the persecution of recent years has forced the leaders to co-operate for self-preservation, so that today, for the first time, there is a united socialist party called the *Shakai-taishuto*. It was able to win eighteen seats in February 1936, and increased this to thirty-seven in April 1937.

THE PEOPLE

Although according to Japanese political theory there is a clear distinction made between the governors and the governed, it is not to be supposed that the common folk of Japan, namely, those who are neither aristocrats, bureaucrats, militarists, nor politicians, are without a voice as to how the government shall be run. In the first place, all men aged twenty-five years or more who have a permanent residence have been eligible to vote in national and local elections since 1925. Thus, the people have some control over the politicians. Since the politicians have so little power, however, this does not mean a great deal. Consequently, the people do not prize their votes highly, and are frequently willing to sell them to the highest bidder. This means that

hood suffrage in 1925 that the mass parties, as such, could engage in organizational campaigns. The Communist party is illegal and subject to continual and ruthless persecution. Its political influence is apparently negligible.

the government in power has an excellent chance
to win the next election, for through the Minister
of Home Affairs, to whom all prefectural governors
and all chiefs of police are politically responsible,
the opposition's campaigning can be seriously cur-
tailed, the polls can be controlled to a large extent,
bribery can be punished severely when engaged in
by others, but winked at when the party's members
make use of it. All in all there is little excuse for
losing an election. The common saying that "The
Government always wins the election" has proved
to be wrong very rarely. Governments resign in
Japan not because they lose elections, but because
they lose the support of some powerful group of the
aristocrats, bureaucrats, or militarists.

1. *Local Government*

Although the common people have a larger voice
in local politics than in national affairs, the prefectural and city assemblies are subservient to the executive authorities, who in turn are the loyal henchmen of the central administration. The executive
veto is virtually unlimited, and the Minister of
Home Affairs can dissolve any recalcitrant local legislature. Government is completely centralized; all
important and many relatively trivial decisions affecting local areas are settled by the Tokyo authorities. There is no conflict of jurisdiction between the
local and central governments, because the former is
no more than a detailed ramification of some division of the latter. Here again one meets with the
Japanese passion for unity.

2. *The Press*

In addition to their vote, the common people have
a second potential instrument of control in the press.

Modern newspapers made their appearance in 1871, but freedom of the press, as it exists in Anglo-Saxon countries, has never been known in Japan. All newspapers or magazines that publish political information must deposit with the government a certain amount of money to cover the payment of anticipated fines. In times of particularly severe press control, important newspapers carry jail editors whose sole duty it is to serve out sentences imposed by the irate authorities. Newspapers have to file with the government the minutest details concerning their organization and policies. Periodically, the authorities flatly ban the printing of information they wish to keep from the people. There were fifty-eight such taboo subjects from January 1935 to May 1936, ranging from foreign policy to cases of rape. "Politics is synonymous with ethics," and the people must not learn what is not good for them to know. Radical newspapers are soon suppressed or persecuted into a state of bankruptcy. Thus, newspapers must content themselves with sly digs at the government and veiled hints that all is not well, or pour vehement invectives on the head of some mediocre bureaucrat or politician for having made some relatively trivial mistake, thereby implying a criticism of the policies or interests with which he is associated.

Nor is there much freedom of assembly or freedom of speech. People may meet together and talk, but not in a spirit of opposition to the existing political and economic order. Such disunity of ideology is not to be tolerated. Those who cease to act as loyal and true subjects should, are swiftly punished. There is no *Habeas Corpus* act. A suspect may be detained almost indefinitely, nor may he claim any "right of counsel." What one reads or with whom one talks may easily become the cause of one's arrest. Thoughts lead to action, and to prevent dangerous actions the government must suppress dangerous thoughts.

3. *Protagonists of Direct Action*

Since the common people can exert but a negligible amount of influence on the government through voting and through the press, those who are dissatisfied with the *status quo* and sincerely desirous of change, join various societies and groups, most of them public, but a few secret, which believe in direct action. Some of the best known are the Communists, the Black Dragon and the Black Ocean Societies, mentioned before, the Imperial League of Young Officers, the "God-sent Troops," and the "Blood Brotherhood." If these groups resort to murder to bring about a change, it is because they believe there is no other line of action open to them. Any action that is strictly legal is bound to be harmless, else it would not long remain legal. Terrorism is the price that the authoritarian regime must pay for refusing to permit peaceful change. Thus far the aristocrats, bureaucrats, and militarists have preferred to run the risk of assassination individually rather than to relinquish their power collectively to elect representatives of the people.

THE CABINET

The battleground of the aristocrats, bureaucrats, militarists, and politicians is the Cabinet (*Naikaku*), for despite the existence of the many powerful organs of the government already mentioned, the Cabinet is still the most important political body in the state, and the Premier the most powerful single figure. Consequently, control of the Cabinet is necessary to any group that desires to enforce some program or policy of its own upon the country.

The Cabinet is not mentioned in the Constitution of 1889, but Article LV declares: "The respective Ministers of State shall give their advice to the Emperor, and be responsible for it.

"All Laws, Imperial Ordinances, and Imperial Rescripts of whatever kind, that relate to the affairs of the State, require the countersignature of a Minister of State."

1. *The Ministers*

The term "Ministers of State" definitely refers to the members of the Cabinet, for a cabinet system was established by an Imperial Ordinance in 1885, four years before the Constitution was promulgated. Moreover, the last article of the Constitution reads in part: "Existing legal enactments, such as laws, regulations, ordinances, or by whatever names they may be called, shall, so far as they do not conflict with the present Constitution, continue in force." Since there was nothing in the Constitution prohibiting the organization of a cabinet, this article recognized the existence and legality of this important organ of the government. Today the cabinet consists of a Premier and twelve Ministers, namely: the Ministers of Foreign Affairs, Home Affairs, Finance, War, the Navy, Justice, Education, Commerce and Industry, Agriculture and Forestry, Communications, Railways, and Overseas Affairs.

The Emperor, upon the recommendation of the Elder Statesmen (*Genro*) and frequently with the advice of the Lord Keeper of the Privy Seal and the Minister of the Imperial Household, commands some prominent figure in political life to form a

Cabinet.[10] If he feels sufficiently sure of the support of a majority from the aristocracy, the bureaucracy, and the militarists, the newly appointed Premier proceeds to select his twelve Ministers. If, with the addition of his twelve confreres, he still manages to command the support of a majority, then a new Government has come into being.

At first the theory was that each man was responsible individually to the Emperor, and that there was no such thing as joint responsibility; that soon proved impractical, and at present the Cabinet generally operates as a unit under the control of the Premier. The exceptions to this rule are the Ministers of War and the Navy. Their special status has been discussed.

Cabinets may be overthrown in many ways. They do not have to possess a majority in the House of Representatives, but should that body impeach the Cabinet or pass a vote of no confidence, the Cabinet resigns. Generally, however, the Premier will request the Emperor to dissolve the House before it has a chance to voice so strong a criticism of the government. The Cabinet will fall if either of the Service Ministers withdraw for any reason and no officer is proffered in his place. Cabinets can be de-

[10] Premiers are not, as is often thought in the West, *chosen* by the *Genro*. It has been the custom that the Emperor should respect above all else the advice of those who were primarily responsible for the rise of the modern Japanese Government. It has been, therefore, principally on their recommendation that all Prime Ministers have been selected. During *Kensei-no-Jodo* ("the period of normal government" from the end of the World War until the Manchurian incident in 1931) the recommendation of the *Genro* was not primary, for the head of, or the choice of, the majority party became Premier more or less automatically. As it happened, Prince Saionji(K), the sole surviving *Genro*, is a liberal and has consistently adopted a favorable attitude towards party Governments.

stroyed by an irate House of Peers or by a Privy
Council that has quarreled with it. Sometimes Cabinets resign in the face of a storm of public criticism coupled with rioting and mob violence. Several
Cabinets have come to an end because of successful
or attempted assassinations of Premiers and important Ministers.

The Cabinet is responsible primarily to the Emperor, however, and only secondarily to the Diet
and the other organs of the government. The Premier and his Ministers need not be, and generally
are not, members of the majority party in the
House of Representatives. From the first meeting
of the Diet in 1890 until June 1898 the premiership
was passed back and forth among the three Elder
Statesmen, Ito(C), Matsukata(S), and Yamagata
(C). From June 1898 to October 1918 semiparty
cabinets made their appearance at intervals, but
only because the *Genro* and their henchmen, such
as Okuma(H), Ito(C), Saionji(K), Katsura(C),
and Yamamoto Gombei(S), found it convenient to
have the backing of the majority party in the Lower
House, and hence accepted the presidency for the
time being of one or another of the major parties.

2. *Party Government*

True party cabinets did not appear until Mr.
Hara, president of the *Seiyukai*, and the first real
"party boss," took office as Premier in the fall of
1918. He was assassinated in 1921 and was succeeded
by Mr. Takahashi, the new president of the *Seiyukai*,
who remained Premier until June 1922. Then came
another period of nonparty cabinets under Admiral
Kato(B), Admiral Yamamoto Gombei(S), and

Count Kiyoura, although these Premiers tried to keep on good terms with at least one powerful party in the Lower House. The heyday of party cabinets began in June 1924, when Kato Takaaki, the brother-in-law of Baron Iwasaki—head of the Mitsubishi interests—became Premier with the backing of both the *Kenseikai* and the *Seiyukai*; and continued through his second premiership and those of Wakatsuki, General Tanaka, Hamaguchi, and Inukai. It was this period from 1924 to May 1932, that made Western liberals believe that constitutional democratic government had come to stay in Japan. Yet eight years is a very short time, and even these eight years were nothing of which party cabinets could boast. General Tanaka, an avowed militarist and advocate of a "strong China policy," was Premier from April 1927 to July 1929; his presidency of the *Seiyukai* did it no good. Then Premier Hamaguchi, president of the *Minseito*, was shot in 1930 and so seriously injured that he died the following year. Premier Wakatsuki succeeded him but was overthrown two months after the outbreak of the Manchurian Incident of September 1931. Finally, Premier Inukai, president of the *Seiyukai*, was assassinated by young army officers on May 15, 1932. Thus, even in the brightest periods of party government, the party cabinets had two of their five premiers assassinated; a third was an out-and-out militarist, and a fourth was unable to prevent the outbreak of the Manchurian Affair and the utter destruction of his conciliatory policy toward China. Since May 1932 the premiership has been in the hands of nonparty bureaucrats such as Hirota Koki, and particularly in the hands of militarists, such as

Admirals Saito and Okada, and General Hayashi. Now it is held by the aristocrat, Prince Konoe(K).

Party cabinets, therefore, are still the exception in Japan. This does not mean that the Cabinet can afford wholly to disregard the parties in the Diet. It has been discovered by most premiers that their political careers will suffer unless they can come to some working agreement with the majority party in the Lower House. However, since the Premier, acting in the name of the Emperor, can prorogue the Diet and dissolve the Lower House, he can often intimidate the members into giving him a great deal of unwilling support. Thus, the Cabinet must be looked upon not so much as the highest organ representing the will of the people, but as another political institution manned primarily by aristocrats, bureaucrats, and militarists, offering its services and loyalty to the "autocracy" rather than to the Diet.

The Cabinet does stand out, nevertheless, as the one principal organ of the state that can be, and is, attacked by the people whenever its policies do not meet with public approval. The attack of the liberals upon the present autocratic regime is concentrated on the Cabinet via the House of Representatives. It is because the aristocrats, bureaucrats, and militarists know that the Cabinet is in the "front line trenches" of the autocracy, and is in danger of being captured at intervals by the exponents of democracy, that they are so careful to limit the Cabinet's powers by the other authoritarian bodies that have already been described. Whenever the politicians do win control, the aristocrats operating from the vantage point of the House of Peers; the bureaucrats from the Privy Council; and the Militarists from the Supreme War Council, the General Staff, and the War and Navy Ministries—can often separately, and always collectively, overthrow the Cabinet abruptly, should it pursue policies that meet with their disapproval.

PART II

HOW THE JAPANESE GOVERNMENT FUNCTIONS (1889–1938)

PART II

CHAPTER V

THE ELDER STATESMEN (*GENRO*) IN POWER (1889–1918)

FOR almost thirty years after the granting of the Imperial Constitution, the Elder Statesmen dominated the political scene. They and their staunch henchmen alone held the premiership from the establishment of that office in 1885 until 1918 with the single exception of Okuma(H) who was, himself, one of the leaders of the restoration and has been classified by some with the *Genro*. Ito(C), Kuroda(S), Yamagata(C), Matsukata(S), Ito(C), Matsukata(S), Ito(C), Okuma(H), Yamagata(C), Ito(C), Katsura(C), Saionji(K), Katsura(C), Yamamoto(S), Okuma(H), and Terauchi(C), was the monotonous order in which the premiership passed back and forth among the Elder Statesmen from Satsuma and Choshu and their loyal favorites from those provinces. Saionji, the only descendant of the Court Nobles(K), owed his prominence primarily to his friendship with the great Ito.

The Elder Statesmen also controlled the Privy

Council, as its dominating presidents from its creation in 1889 to the death of Prince Yamagata(C) in 1922, after a tenure of seventeen consecutive years in that office. Only twice was the presidency in other hands than those of the *Genro*, from 1890 to 1892 when Count Oki Takato(H), a fellow clansman of Elder Statesman Okuma Shigenobu, held it, and again from 1895 to 1899 when Count Kuroda Kiyotaka(S) served as president of the Privy Council.

Nor is this the complete picture of the power wielded by the *Genro*. The three most influential men in the history of the Japanese Imperial Army were Field-Marshals Yamagata(C), Oyama(S), and General Katsura(C), all of whom were *Genro*. By the time of Field-Marshal Prince Yamagata's death in 1922 practically every important officer in the Imperial Japanese Army was indebted at least indirectly to him for his promotions; when this *Genro* spoke the army promptly obeyed. No such figure has risen to fill his place, which explains in large part the appearance of factions within the army since Prince Yamagata's death, and the army's consequent lapses from discipline, as for example, the rebellion of February 26, 1936.

Prince Matsukata(S), to a lesser degree, could rely upon the navy to be obedient to his will, since this Elder Statesman was from the Satsuma clan, which openly ruled the Imperial Japanese Navy for many years, and does to some extent even today. Field-Marshal Oyama also was a Satsuma man, as were Admiral Yamamoto Gombei and Count Kuroda Kiyotaka, so that the *Genro* and their henchmen had the navy safely under their control.

These "eight old men"—seven were *samurai* of

Satsuma or Choshu, and the eighth a Court Noble
(*Kuge*)—were the actual rulers of Japan from be-
fore 1885 down to the death of Field-Marshal Prince
Yamagata in 1922. Only twenty-nine men held the
posts of Premier, Lord Keeper of the Privy Seal,
Minister of the Imperial Household, Minister of
War, Minister of the Navy, President of the Privy
Council, and President of the House of Peers from
1885 to 1918. Of these, twenty-two came from the
five groups that had brought about the Imperial
Restoration. Seven were *samurai* from Satsuma,[1]
four from Choshu,[2] three from Hizen,[3] two from
Tosa,[4] five were Court Nobles(*Kuge*),[5] and one,
Tokugawa Iesato, would have been the next *Shogun*.
Of the seven "outsiders"[6] Fleet-Admiral Kato
Tomosaburo was considered the right-hand man of
Fleet-Admiral Togo Heihachiro, the great Satsuma
samurai who became the chief naval hero of modern
Japan; Lieutenant-General Oshima Ken'ichi had
served a long time under Field-Marshal Prince
Yamagata; and Hachisuka Mochiaki was the ex-
Daimyo of Tokushima in Awa, and had married into
the Tokugawa family. Thus, the old guard of pre-
constitutional days carried on throughout the next
thirty years under the aegis of the Satsuma and

[1] Kuroda Kiyotaka, Matsukata Masayoshi, Yamamoto Gombei, Oyama Iwao, Saigo Tsugumichi, Kabayama Sukenori, Nire
Kagenori.
[2] Ito Hirobumi, Yamagata Aritomo, Katsura Taro, Terauchi
Seiki.
[3] Okuma Shigenobu, Oki Takato, Hatano Yoshino.
[4] Tanaka Mitsuaki, Hijikata Hisamoto, Itagaki Taisuke, perhaps the best-known member of the Tosa faction, held other
offices.
[5] Saionji Kimmochi, Sanjo Saneyoshi, Tokudaiji Sanenori, Iwakura Tomosada, Konoe Atsumaro.
[6] Saito Makoto, Yashiro Rokuro, Kato Tomosaburo, Watanabe
Chiaki, Hachisuka Mochiaki, Oka Ichinosuke, Oshima Ken'ichi.

Choshu *Genro*. It will merit detailed study to learn how the new organs of government functioned under such leadership.

CONSTITUTIONAL GOVERNMENT BEGINS, 1889

Elder Statesman Ito(C) resigned the premiership and the presidency of the Privy Council in 1889 shortly after the new constitution had been promulgated, as he had then completed his work for the time. This action was part of an agreement made between the Satsuma and Choshu leaders. He was succeeded as Premier by Kuroda Kiyotaka(S), who is sometimes counted among the Elder Statesmen. Kuroda's Cabinet fell after Foreign Minister Okuma (H) had his leg blown off by a bomb thrown by a person who desired to express opposition to the government's policy regarding the "unequal treaties." Neither Ito(C) nor Elder Statesman Inoue(C) cared to assume the unpleasant duty of facing the antagonistic members of the new House of Representatives that was to meet in 1890 for the first time. Finally, Elder Statesman Yamagata(C), a blunt soldier with a *samurai's* contempt for the bourgeoisie and democratic institutions, was persuaded to serve as Premier.

There were nine political parties, but the *Jiyuto* under Itagaki(T) and the *Kaishinto* under Okuma (H) won one hundred and seventy of the three hundred seats, Itagaki's party being much the stronger with one hundred and thirty to Okuma's forty. These two men were the acknowledged leaders of the opposition as they still felt bitter toward the Satsuma-Choshu clique for monopolizing the key positions in the new regime. The government, being afraid of too close co-operation between hostile parties, had passed a law earlier in the year prohibiting the amalgamation of parties until the original organizations concerned had been completely dissolved. This helped to make co-operation between the opposition groups difficult.

The Satsuma-Choshu government had no party support. With Elder Statesman Ito(C) as President of the House of Peers, and in complete control of that body, any disagreeable legislation passed by the House of Representatives could easily be killed in the Upper House. The members of the Lower House poured out a stream of abusive criticism under the supervision of Itagaki(T) and Okuma(H), cut the budget by ten million *yen*, and made themselves generally disagreeable to the haughty authorities. The House of Peers, however, prevented any serious legislation from being passed, and after various compromises were made, the first session came to an end without a dissolution or a vote of no confidence.

THE DIET DEFIES THE OLIGARCHY

Yamagata resigned as Premier in 1891 as he was dissatisfied with the progress made in treaty revision and had no inclination for another fight with the Diet. He was succeeded by Elder Statesman Matsukata(S). This passing of the premiership back and forth among the Elder Statesmen enraged the parties under Okuma(H) and Itagaki(T), who demanded that cabinets responsible to the Diet be formed. Since the government refused to countenance such a proposal, these two men proceeded systematically to make the Constitution of 1889 unworkable. Immediately on convening at the close of 1891 in its second session, the Lower House attacked the government on almost every point, fought the budget, and drowned all business in a torrent of vituperative oratory. Elder Statesman Inoue(C) was accused by Okuma of amassing a fortune through serving the interests of the Mitsui family; Okuma, however, was doing the same by promoting the Mitsubishi interests of the Iwasaki family. The government became so disgusted that it dissolved the House of Representatives on Christmas Day, after it had rejected the naval estimates. Okuma(H) and Itagaki (T) looked upon this as a triumph, for the government was thus compelled to adopt the budget of the preceding year.

The election held in February 1892 was bitterly contested. Matsukata's(S) government was determined to win at any cost, and it put up candidates in every district. The prefectural governors and chiefs of police were instructed by the Minister of Home Affairs to control the election in such a way as to return these candidates. The parties were furious. In the ensuing riots, which were actually pitched battles in Itagaki's native province of Tosa, twenty-five were killed and three hundred and eighty-eight injured. Moreover, the government won only ninety-five seats. The oligarchy had definitely been beaten, but Matsukata refused to resign. When the Diet met in May a crisis soon developed between the two Houses over the question of a supplementary budget, the Lower House claiming precedence over the Upper House in such matters. Finally, an appeal was made to the Emperor for an interpretation of the constitution on this point. The answer was delivered after the Privy Council had settled the point, the statement being that both Houses had equal powers in financial matters.

The Government weathered the session, but it was so cordially hated that the Matsukata Cabinet resigned shortly afterward. Itagaki(T) and Okuma (H) were well pleased, since now both Yamagata(C) and Matsukata(S) had been driven from office. They waited impatiently for Ito(C) and Inoue(C) to place themselves in a position to suffer the same fate.

THE OLIGARCHY DEFIES THE DIET

Ito(C) took the premiership and attempted to placate public opinion by dismissing eleven of the worst offenders among the prefectural governors. However, the Lower House was still in a belligerent mood when it convened for the fourth session late in 1892. It reduced the ordinary expenditures listed in the budget by eight million *yen* and dropped out a three million, three hundred and thirty-three thousand *yen* item that was to be annual installment on an extraordinary fund for building battleships. The Cabinet refused to accept these cuts. The Diet sent an Address to the Throne and adjourned for eighteen days. It was summoned almost immediately to hear an Imperial Rescript informing it that it had no power to change fixed expenditures as it was trying to do. In addition, a statement was issued in the Sovereign's name that read, "We direct Our military and civil officials, except in cases where special circumstances interfere, to contribute one-tenth of their salaries during the same period (i.e., period of the annual special expenditures on the navy), which sums shall be devoted to supplement the fund for building men-of-war." In this manner, Premier Ito not only won the budget he wanted, but compelled the members of the opposition to contribute to the naval fund. The Diet was thoroughly defeated, and the session ended peacefully.

The fifth session of the Diet was another stormy one. Premier Ito(C) had won some support from Itagaki's(T) *Jiyuto*, but had thereby offended the House of Peers for having made an alliance with a despised political party. Okuma(H) and his loyal *Kaishinto* supporters were out to revenge themselves for the defeat of the previous session, and made political capital out of some unsavory Stock Exchange scandals to send an Address to the Throne on the subject of official discipline. Premier Ito felt compelled to resign, but the oligarchy struck back through a message from the Emperor, which declared that "the appointment or removal of Ministers of State is absolutely at the will of the Sovereign, and no interference is allowed in this matter." Ito was ordered by himself and his fellow Elder Statesmen to resume the premiership. Thereupon Okuma's party shifted the attack to a condemnation of his foreign policy. The Diet was then prorogued for ten days, then for fourteen, and finally dissolved for the second time on December 30, 1893.

The election following in March was again a bloody affair. One person was killed and some one hundred and fifty injured. The government made use of its strict Press Law and Law of Public Meetings to harass the opposition, and was at least able to cut their majority to some extent. The special session of the Diet convened in May. The government was immediately impeached for having dissolved the Diet in the preceding December. An Address to the Throne was carried. Then the oligarchy struck back. The Emperor refused to accept the message, so that the President of the House of Representatives had to leave it with the Minister of the Imperial Household. He was informed through this person that the

Emperor would make no reply, because he would not receive the Address. Before the Diet could recover from this surprise, it was dissolved for the third time in six sessions.

WAR UNITES THE FACTIONS, 1894

Things had now reached an impasse. The Satsuma-Choshu oligarchs still refused to grant the Lower House any control over the cabinet, but Okuma's(H) and Itagaki's(T) followers were in turn bringing the wheels of government almost to a standstill by preventing the passage of any legislation. Obviously, something had to be done. Ito, at this juncture, decided to join the group that was clamoring for war with China. There was no doubt but that the people wanted a dynamic, spectacular foreign policy. It was also apparent that the existing stalemate had to be broken. So Ito reversed the decision he had made in 1873, when he had urged peace instead of war, and encouraged the outbreak of hostilities between Japan and China.

Immediately the nation rose to the support of the administration. The election in September was very peaceful, and the new Diet passed, without a murmer of disapproval, huge special and emergency budgets. Later, to show its patriotism, it passed a unanimous resolution to vote any sum of money the government needed for carrying on the war. But Ito found that internal peace was at the cost of his own influence in the government, for he was a civilian and with the advent of war his fellow clansman and Elder Statesman, Yamagata(C), the great soldier, began to overshadow him in the councils of the oligarchy. Both Yamagata and Elder Statesman Oyama(S) won great reputations as heads of the two expeditionary forces, but Ito did not. Even worse, as Premier, after negotiation of the Treaty of Shimonoseki, he was principally instrumental in accepting the "advice" of Russia, France, and Germany to return the Liaotung Peninsula to China. This made him probably the most unpopular man in Japan for the moment, as the people had expected to gain a great deal from the war and were bitterly disappointed at the meagerness of the fruits of victory. Taxes had to be increased to meet the new expense of enlarged armaments since Japan was now brought face to face with Russia.

DISCORD PREVAILS AGAIN

When the Diet met again in December following the signing of the treaty, Ito was bitterly attacked by Okuma's *Kaishinto*. Ito, however, had made some deal with Itagaki's *Jiyuto* and other groups and thus controlled a majority, so that his cabinet was able to survive the session.

Early in 1896 Okuma founded a new party called the *Shimpoto* which was made up of the old *Kaishinto* members and some fifty others. When Ito saw that he would have a majority of the Diet against him, he resigned. His power was now definitely on the wane and Okuma's star was ascending. Elder Statesman Matsukata(S) took the premiership and made Okuma Minister of Foreign Affairs in return for his support in the Diet, promising that the Cabinet would soon be made responsible to the Lower House. Just as a working agreement had been made between the Choshu oligarchs under Ito's leadership and Itagaki's *Jiyuto*, so now the Satsuma oligarchs under Matsukata and the members of Okuma's *Shimpoto* attempted to co-operate. But the party men soon found Matsukata's promise to be an empty one. Okuma resigned as Minister of Foreign Affairs, and the *Shimpoto* joined the *Jiyuto* in opposing the administration. In December 1897 the Diet passed a vote of no confidence; it was dissolved the same day for the fourth time. Matsukata's resignation as Premier followed immediately.

Ito(C) then formed a Cabinet with Elder Statesmen Inoue(C), Saionji(K), and Katsura(C) as members. In the ensuing election Itagaki's *Jiyuto* won ninety-nine seats and Okuma's *Shimpoto* won one hundred and five out of a total of three hundred. Both were still bitter against the Satsuma-Choshu oligarchy and defeated the government's Land Tax Bill. The Diet was promptly dissolved for the fifth time and the Cabinet resigned.

PARTY GOVERNMENT IS TRIED, 1898

At a meeting of the Elder Statesmen immediately after these events, Ito, seeing that his power was slipping into the hands of the militarists led by Yamagata(C), advocated the establishment of a party cabinet. Yamagata opposed this strenuously, but Ito carried the day. Okuma(H) and Itagaki(T) were ordered to form a cabinet. This was so unexpected that they were taken by surprise. They had dissolved the *Jiyuto* and the *Shimpoto*, and formed a joint party called the *Kenseito*. This party controlled two-thirds of the members of the House of Representatives, so that the prospects for a successful party cabinet were favorable. Okuma became Premier and Itagaki Minister of Foreign Affairs. The militarists in the oligarchy were represented in the Cabinet by Ministers of War Katsura(C) and of the Navy Saigo(S). Ito went to China to investigate various matters, believing that Yamagata had been safely checked by this new coalition cabinet. The general election that summer returned 259 *Kenseito* members to the House, of which 112 were old *Shimpoto* and 96 were old *Jiyuto* members. However, the two parties soon fell to quarreling over the spoils of office, the *Kenseito* broke up, Itagaki's *Jiyuto* members resigned from the Cabinet, and Okuma shortly afterward had to give up the premiership.

Party government had proved a dismal failure the first time it had been attempted. The militarists in the oligarchy were delighted. Before Ito could get back from China, Yamagata had formed a new government in which no party members nor persons of the Ito faction in the oligarchy held a cabinet post.

The old *Jiyuto* group under Itagaki kept the name *Kenseito*, while Okuma's *Shimpoto* members formed a party called the true *Kenseito* or *Kensei-honto*. Yamagata came to a working agreement with Itagaki's party and was thereby able to command a majority of the Lower House. Yamagata had utter contempt for the party politicians, but he knew that their votes were necessary. Consequently, he gave them bribes and offices in exchange for their support of his demands for larger sums for the army and the navy.

YAMAGATA DEFINES WAR MINISTRY QUALIFICATIONS

It was during his premiership that Yamagata rather surreptitiously appended a list of persons eligible to hold the posts of Ministers of War and the Navy as a supplement to the Imperial Ordinances for the organization of the two military departments. Only active generals and lieutenant-generals, and active admirals and vice-admirals were placed on this list. Since the nation was busily engaged in preparing for the coming war with Russia, and it was considered but reasonable that professional soldiers well acquainted with the armed forces should head those two ministries, no particular attention was paid to the political significance of such an arrangement. In this inconspicuous manner, Elder Statesman Yamagata, a strong militarist and opponent of the political parties, placed the Cabinet at the mercy of the Ministers for the armed forces. The army and the navy have been taking advantage of this situation ever since.

Yamagata was interested in increasing the taxation on land, to obtain more money for military expenditures. This was impossible so long as the Diet members were predominantly from the rural districts. The *Kenseito* and *Kensei-honto* were strongest in the urban areas, hence they too had reasons for wanting larger representation from the cities. Consequently, Yamagata found himself for once in spontaneous agreement with a Diet majority and a new election law was passed increasing the membership of the House from 300 to 381 and the electorate from some 500,000 to about a million.

ITO FORMS A SEIYUKAI PARTY CABINET, 1900

The House of Peers was angered by Yamagata's alliance with the *Kenseito* and defeated some government bills to show its displeasure. Ito returned from China, bitter against Yamagata for having supplanted him as the leading oligarch, and made speeches throughout the country advocating party government in the hope that he might break the militarist section of the Satsuma-Choshu clique thereby. The *Kenseito*, finding that Yamagata was simply using it as a despised although necessary tool, and hoping to receive more from Ito, withdrew its support from the government, dissolved the party and formed a new one called the *Seiyukai*, with Ito as the president. One hundred and fifty-two members of the Diet eagerly joined this party.

The *Kensei-honto*, becoming concerned over the increasing prestige of its rival, made Okuma the official head of the party once more. Yamagata resigned as Premier late in 1900, because he did not care to face a Diet in which the *Seiyukai* under Ito would have an absolute majority. He knew that nothing seriously opposed to his plans could be done by any government, now that he and his fellow militarists in the oligarchy had absolute control of the Ministries of War and the Navy. He was succeeded as Premier by his rival oligarch, Ito, the civilian, who formed a Cabinet solely of *Seiyukai* members with the exception of Minister of Foreign Affairs Kato Takaaki—brother-in-law of Baron Iwasaki, the head of the Mitsubishi interests, and Ministers of War Katsura(C) and the Navy Yamamoto Gombei(S).

At the next session of the Diet the government introduced a bill calling for new taxes to supply money which the armed forces needed in preparing for war against Russia. Many of the *Seiyukai* members were opposed to the bill, but when Ito threatened to resign, the bill was passed and sent to the House of Peers. There it was soundly defeated as the Peers were angry at Ito for having accepted the presidency of a political party, and the *Seiyukai* members had been talking openly about reforming

the Upper House. Then suddenly came a bolt from
the blue in the form of an Imperial Message to the
House of Peers ordering it to accept the bill. The
Peers did, but they were so angry at Ito for his use
of the Emperor against them that they passed all
the other legislation submitted to them during the
remainder of the session without bothering to discuss or even read it. The unprecedented feature
about this Imperial Message was that it bore no
countersignature of any Minister of State. Ito vowed
he had nothing to do with it, and it is possible that
Yamagata may have caused it to be sent in order to
place Ito in an embarrassing position, and because
Yamagata wanted the money for the army and navy.
Ito, whether he deserved it or not, received the
blame for the episode and became highly unpopular
with the country at large. He was quite chagrined,
resigned his office, and asked that he be stripped of
his titles and his rank, but his request was refused
and he was ordered to remain as Premier. Shortly
afterward, Ito quarreled with the *Seiyukai* over his
Minister of Finance and finally in May 1901 he resigned in disgust. This was his last attempt to rule
the country as Premier and marked the final collapse
of the civilian wing of the oligarchy. Yamagata was
asked to form a cabinet, but refused, as he knew Ito
and the *Seiyukai* would welcome the opportunity to
attack him. Ito's friend, Inoue(C), the other important civilian Elder Statesman, was then offered the
premiership, but he had to admit that he was unable
to form a Government. Then the militarist, Kat-
sura(C), was asked but he declined. Ito was next
offered the post, but had to turn it down. All this
was very humiliating to him and Inoue. Finally,

Katsura consented to form a cabinet, saying that he was perfectly neutral, neither favoring nor opposing political parties.

At the Diet session in December 1901 the *Seiyukai* and Okuma's *Kensei-honto* opposed the Government's budget. Katsura(C) then had to come to terms with the *Seiyukai* in order to get the budget through the Lower House. Shortly after, the *Seiyukai* quarrelled violently with the House of Peers. The Upper House declared that parties were an abomination and the *Seiyukai* called the Peers an anachronism and utterly useless to the government. However, both the Cabinet and the Diet survived the session.

These particular members of the Lower House having served four years, a general election was held in the summer of 1902. The *Seiyukai* won 190 seats and the *Shimpoto*—the *Kensei-honto* had reverted to its earlier name—took 105. The new Diet met in December and promptly refused to pass the government's new Land Tax Bill. The Diet was suspended for five days, then prorogued for seven more days. Undaunted, when it met again it defeated the bill. The Government retaliated by dissolving the Lower House for the sixth time, and the budget of the preceding year automatically went into effect. Premier Katsura knew that the Diet members were opposed to increases in taxes, but he reasoned that men who had spent between two thousand and six thousand *yen* for their seats would not care to lose them before they had had a chance to draw some salary and to reap a reward in bribes and commissions from interests to whom their votes were of value.

WAR WITH RUSSIA APPROACHES

The ensuing election early in 1903 saw Ito's *Seiyukai* with 193 seats to 91 for Okuma's *Shimpoto*. Ito realized that war with Russia was imminent, and that the armed forces had to get their money. He therefore threatened to resign as head of the party if the *Seiyukai* members continued to defeat Premier Katsura's taxation bill. Consequently, the bill was passed over the *Shimpoto's* strenuous opposition, but it nearly wrecked the *Seiyukai* which now showed pronounced signs of disintegration. Ito resigned and turned over the presidency of the party to his political protégé, Saionji Kimmochi(K), a liberal and firm believer in party government. Yamagata(C) and Katsura(C) had Ito elevated to the Presidency of the Privy Council in order to make sure that his break with the *Seiyukai* would be a permanent one.

The next regular session of the Diet was in December 1903. It was customary for the President of the Lower House to give a stereotyped reply to the Emperor's Message opening the Diet. This was a mere formality to which the Diet members paid little attention. This particular president, however, was bitterly opposed to what he considered a weak foreign policy; he put the regular speech prepared for him by the Chief Secretary in his pocket, drew out his own address, and read it off rapidly. The members were not listening and let it pass. It proved to be an impeachment of the Cabinet, which promptly replied by dissolving the Diet for the seventh time. The public was surprised, but pleased at the President's audacity. However, many of the Diet members were highly annoyed at losing their seats again.

Two months later war broke out with Russia, and all domestic quarrels were forgotten. The Diet members vied with each other in proclaiming their loyalty to the government. But on the signing of the highly unpopular Treaty of Portsmouth in 1905, the government was bitterly attacked once more. Newspapers even advocated assassinating some of the oligarchs. There were riots, and martial law had to be proclaimed. Because Katsura(C) did not want to face so hostile a Diet, he resigned in favor of Saionji(K), president of the *Seiyukai*. Ito(C) went to Korea as Resident-General, determined to prevent annexation, which was what Yamagata wanted, and which would undoubtedly mean that a military man would replace Ito.

ITO FAILS TO BLOCK THE ANNEXATION OF KOREA

The Saionji Cabinet held power until 1908. The Diet members having managed to serve out a full four-year term, a general election was held in May 1908. Saionji's *Seiyukai* won 189 seats giving it an absolute majority for the first time. The Cabinet's financial policy, however, met with the disapproval of the military group in the oligarchy, which decided it was time for Saionji to resign. Consequently Saionji resigned, on the grounds of ill health, and recommended Katsura(C) as his successor. Ito's position as Resident-General of Korea was now quite insecure because Katsura and Yamagata were determined to annex the country. In 1909 Ito was removed from office and a satellite of Katsura was put in his place, but Ito still had enough influence to block annexation of Korea. He was sent on a tour of

Korea and Manchuria, and at Harbin he was assassinated by a Korean.

The popular indignation at Ito's assassination made the work of the expansionists easy, and the statesman's death became the very instrument of that which he had striven so long to obstruct. The militarists were able to bring Korea into the Empire in the following year, 1910. Ito's assassination was a truly miserable end for a man who had probably wielded more influence in Japanese political history than any other person of his generation. After Ito's death Yamagata's control of the oligarchy was unquestioned. He was the real ruler of Japan until 1922 when he died.

Meanwhile, the Diet was rather docile in Katsura's hands, as it was busily engaged in making up the heavy financial losses incurred during the election year of 1908. Not by connection with Saionji and the Government, but by great expenditure of money, the *Seiyukai* had gained a majority in the election of the previous May. A scandal in which many *Seiyukai* members were involved was disclosed when the Japan Sugar Refining Company, set up in 1906, became bankrupt in 1909. It was found that more than a million *yen* of its looted capital had been spent in bribing Diet members in 1907 and 1908. Many Diet members therefore wished to avoid any overfastidiousness in examining the conduct of the Government.

By 1910, however, the loss had been made up, and the scandal had blown over. The Diet began to drive hard bargains with Katsura. Terauchi Seiki, who had been Minister of War since 1902, was made Resident-General of Korea, and in August 1910 Korea was annexed. Katsura, tired of the irritating struggle with the Diet, voluntarily resigned in the fall of 1911; and the oligarchy returned Saionji to power, with a Cabinet that included three members of the *Seiyukai*. In May 1912, the Diet having completed its third four-year term in succession, general elections were held again and the *Seiyukai* increased their majority. There were fewer dissolutions during this period, as both the oligarchs and the politicians were playing the game together. The former might have the power, but they paid the Diet well for the privilege of wielding it.

THE MEIJI ERA ENDS, 1912

On July 30, 1912 the Meiji Emperor died. Many of his old statesmen considered this the symbolic death of their whole generation. Nogi, the Hero of Port Arthur, committed suicide together with his wife; it seemed useless, if not even wrong, to outlive their Sovereign. A great epoch had ended, and only a few outstanding men were left to carry on the affairs of the nation. Matsukata and Inoue were old and tired. Yamagata was still the most powerful figure, guiding Premier Saionji in all he did.

Shortly after the inauguration of the new era of *Taisho* (Great Righteousness), Japan experienced a cabinet crisis that was at once the basic symptom of the disease from which the government has not yet ceased to suffer, and the signal for the only serious attempt to uproot the powerful Yamagata from his dominating position in the State. The Army had been insisting for some time on the creation of two new divisions for Korean service, and when, in December 1912, it became evident that Saionji, backed by the civilians in his Cabinet, intended to persist in his opposition, War Minister General Uyehara resigned.

Refusing to accept the principle that the resignation of one member should mean the destruction of a cabinet, Saionji sought anxiously for another War Minister, but Yamagata's plan to keep military control of the nation worked well. Only a General or a Lieutenant-General in active service might hold the portfolio, and the Army, under Yamagata's control, refused to appoint any of its members. Saionji's Cabinet fell; he was commanded to place himself at the service of his Emperor as a *Genro*, the last such appointment made; and the power of the militarists, to the complete extension of which he was later to become a major obstacle, was ominously assured.

The premiership was offered in turn to Inoue(C), Matsukata(S), Yamagata(C), and Terauchi(C). Angered, the various parties joined forces in denouncing the oligarchs for having broken the cabinet. At the end of the month, General Katsura finally organized a Government.

KATSURA ATTEMPTS TO IGNORE YAMAGATA

Katsura(C) had been alternating as Premier with Saionji(K), and when his last cabinet had resigned in 1911, he had gone to Europe. Upon the very day of his return, shortly after the Emperor's death, Yamagata had secured for him appointment as Court Chamberlain and Lord Keeper of the Privy Seal. Aware that this must appear as though it were a promotion out of politics, and quite sensible of Yamagata's coolness toward him, which had been increasing since the 1908-1911 Cabinet, Katsura made a public proclamation that he was quitting politics forever to devote his life to his young Emperor.

Katsura once had been Yamagata's protégé, but by 1912 they were rivals. In the preceding year Katsura had had himself made a Prince; he had already acquired a huge fortune. Not without reason, Yamagata feared for his own security as the head of the army, and though both of them were Choshu men, it became evident that he was doing all in his power to drive Katsura from his high place in clan councils.

To return to December 1912, the capital was suddenly astounded by an Imperial Edict ordering Katsura to resign his court offices and enter politics once more. He accepted the premiership and at once attacked the problem of forming a new cabinet. At the same time another edict was issued, compelling Admiral Saito to retain his office as Minister of the Navy. These steps undoubtedly were personal victories for Katsura over Yamagata and clan government.[7]

The new Premier, however, was unpopular. The people were angry at the debts the army was piling up. The Navy, under Saito, took advantage of the situation to obtain appropriations for fleet expansion. The Diet was hostile to Katsura on general principles, and adjourned until January 20, 1913, refusing then the Government request to extend the recess until February 5. On January 21 the Diet wanted to know who had put Katsura in the premiership while he was holding court offices, and who had told the young Emperor to keep Admiral Saito in control of the navy; the Diet was at once prorogued for two weeks. On the same day Katsura launched what was to be his master stroke: a new party, the Constitutional Fellow-thinkers' Society (*Rikken Doshikai*).

---

[7] His War Minister, be it noted, was Kigoshi Yasutsuna, a *samurai* of Kaga, in the north of Japan—not a Choshu man.

Friends of the popular cause were warmly urged to associate themselves with this new friend of popular government. At once the significance of the Imperial Order to Saito became apparent, as well as that of the rescript extricating Katsura himself from the limbo of the court. This action revealed the true situation: he had been ousted from the Choshu clique, and by dint of personal wealth and power was defying both Yamagata and the Satsuma faction.

THE POLITICIANS OVERTHROW KATSURA

Politics' newest recruit used his money well, so that by February 5 he had brought about ninety Diet members under his standard; but these were too few to control the House. Not only did the people in general dislike him, but the parties, delighted as they were to see him defy the oligarchy, banded together against his new party that threatened to harm them.

When the Diet reassembled on February 5, it was promptly prorogued until February 8, then to February 10. When, at this time, it was intimated that it would be prorogued yet again, mobs rioted in the streets of the cities. Katsura, broken, was forced to resign. He died in October. He had defied the *Genro*, the militarists, the parties, and the clans; he had tried by Bismarckian tactics to set himself up in a modern pattern as a dictator. He failed; and with him failed the principal revolt in the governing oligarchy against the domination of Yamagata. He had used the Emperor to gain his own political ends; toward him was directed a burning resentment that united all factions as they could not unite before; he could not have helped but fail.

Three of the *Genro* met again and Admiral Count Yamamoto Gombei of Satsuma was summoned as the next Premier. He was disliked, and when the Diet met and began to inquire into the naval scandals centering about the building of new battleships, riots started once more and troops had to be called out to quiet the mobs. The Lower House cut thirty million *yen* from the naval budget; and then the Peers, angered too, snapped off another seventy million *yen*, which incensed the Lower House and resulted in a quarrel that prevented the passage of any budget. Yamamoto's Cabinet fell on March 23, 1914.

OKUMA HEADS THE WORLD WAR CABINET

Marquis Okuma, Japan's "tribune of the people," finally organized a Cabinet on April 16, after an unsuccessful attempt by Count Kiyoura. Under his Government the army finally received its two new divisions for Korea, though not until after war had been declared on Germany and Kiaochow had been captured.

Meanwhile the Naval scandals continued under Okuma's regime, and though official denials were made, it was generally believed that the removal of Admiral Yamamoto, and Saito, his Navy Minister, from active duty to the reserve list, was closely connected with the whole scandal which had involved the Mitsui firm as well as the English Vickers Company. Excitement did not subside until punishments had been meted out; fines were decreed and in at least one case imprisonment followed.

At the same time, Saionji was resigning as head of the weakened *Seiyukai*, to be succeeded by Hara Kei. New general elections gave 150 seats to the

Doshikai, founded in 1913 by Katsura. It thus became the main party, and in November 1914 it was
joined by other parties to become the *Kenseikai*.

Again, in March 1915, after another general election, the Diet's composition favored Okuma, with
152 members of the *Doshikai* and 59 others supporting him opposed to 138 in the opposition, including
110 members of the *Seiyukai*. In the May Diet meeting Hara of the *Seiyukai* bitterly attacked the government's foreign policy, maintaining that the
Twenty-one Demands had destroyed the traditional
Chinese friendship. In June it was discovered that
the Minister of Home Affairs had bribed the Diet
members to vote for the two army divisions. This
raised such a storm that on July 29 the whole Cabinet tendered its resignation, but dissolution was
avoided by the timely sacrifice of Kato, the Foreign
Minister.

Okuma, meanwhile, was prospering financially by
the war, and was handling his foreign policy well.
Leader Hara of the *Seiyukai*, however, criticized his
every move, and the people began to realize that
Okuma, as Premier, did not deserve all the credit he
was receiving. Finally, in October 1916, Okuma, tired
of it all, resigned, and was succeeded by Terauchi
Seiki, a Yamaguchi *samurai*, at the command of
Yamagata. Okuma was invited by the Emperor to
serve as one of the *Genro*, but consistent with his
often-expressed contempt for that body, he refused
to take this invitation seriously.

RIOTS END THE TERAUCHI CABINET, 1918

In April 1917 in a new general election called because Terauchi was unable to work with the Okuma-
controlled *Kenseikai*, the *Seiyukai*, with which the

new premier now allied himself, emerged generally victorious. Terauchi's new Cabinet found it useful to suppress most of the news that was not favorable to itself, particularly as at this time difficult labor problems were arising. There was a great demand for workers, and rising prices made striking profitable as well as necessary. During this one year there were 398 strikes involving 57,000 workmen.

The next year saw continued labor problems. Rice riots occurred, due to high prices. The city of Kobe witnessed the worst of these, and troops and police were called out to suppress them. Unable to cope *1918* with the situation, the Terauchi Cabinet fell on September 17.

 Hara, the "Great Commoner," came in as the *Seiyukai* Premier. He was the first untitled man to hold this position. Being a staunch party man, and a good politician, he gained the loyalty of the people; there was a feeling in many quarters that the logical conclusion of the trend that politics had been taking was now at last reached, and that party government, as such, had definitely arrived.

CHAPTER VI

THE PARTY POLITICIANS IN POWER
(1918–1932)

In October 1918 Japan faced a new era. The militarist Terauchi had failed; and with the fall of his Cabinet, it was said, the old school was discredited and finished. Age now threatened the autocratic *Genro*, which nothing else had been able to move. The one among them whose life might extend farthest into the new time was Saionji, a liberal. Natural forces had brought their results, and just as the great Western War to Preserve Democracy was ending, Japan too was swinging into line. Triumphantly, liberal observers proclaimed this to be the Period of Normal Government (*Kensei no Jodo*).[1]

Much reason existed, however, for questioning just how normal this government really was, or if normal, how long it would be able to withstand the chronic ailments of Japanese government? Yamagata's years may have been numbered, but he was still very much alive; and as no strong single leader had arisen under him in the army, it was the more to be feared that when his harmonizing influence was gone, the power he had created for the military leadership might be used less circumspectly. Among the party politicians, there was no systematic organization but only temporary obedience to the very few powerful leaders, so

[1] As a technical term, *Kensei no Jodo* includes generally the period of party government from 1918 to 1932.

that if anything happened to its leader—as was three times the case[2]—the party was lost.

BASES OF CONFLICT

The bitter conflict among the several elements of the Japanese government is now clearly seen to have been the inevitable result of the way in which the "democratization" of the governmental structure was attempted. Men, not laws, are the determining element in Japanese politics; and if the party politicians controlled the actual making of the laws, then the men who believed those laws to be harmful to what they conceived as proper interests would, by every rule of an older tradition than that which the politicians worked by, undertake to ignore or subvert such laws. It might be that the politicians would secure eventual victory; but that victory would be controlled by factors going far deeper than the government into the body of the Japanese nation. The mere inauguration of *Kensei no Jodo* did not insure that victory; rather, it made it inevitable that the desperate struggle for the victory could not be far away.

During the period of "the *Genro* in Power," the elements of the Japanese government had taken form and certain conflicts had appeared. Because the leaders had all been great men, however, and of the same upper social stratum, the rivalries had been between men for leadership, for example, Ito and Yamagata, rather than between groups for ideological control, such as the party cabinets and the Privy Council. Formerly, members of the oligarchy had found it convenient to work with one party or another at various

---

[2] Hara (*Seiyukai*), Hamaguchi (*Minseito*), and Inukai (*Seiyukai*) were all assassinated while holding the premiership.

times, just as Bismarck had eventually come to work with parties in Germany. They were responsible exclusively to the Emperor, however, and if they found the majority party obnoxious, they could have it dissolved, and maneuver the ensuing elections in order to secure a majority that would be more pliable. Their closest connections were ordinarily with the Privy Council, the militarists, and the House of Peers; together, they generally treated the Lower House as a nuisance apart, that had to be abided, but which was definitely to be managed. Now, the premier was still responsible directly to the Emperor, but as a logical development from the former system, the premiers were the leaders, or appointees of the majority party. If a premier's party lost its majority in any election—despite the fact that its control of the government gave it a magnificent vote-controlling instrument—then the premier must resign; or if his party denounced him, then he must resign; unless, in either case, he were prepared to end *Kensei no Jodo* by a single stroke and continue in office despite party mandates. There was now, therefore, a definite responsibility of the premier to the majority party in the House of Representatives; and this acted to take the premiership from its former association with the other powerful organs of state, and align it with the despised Diet.

THE PARTY POLITICIANS

The notion of the "Commoners in Power" has been, however, overemphasized. The commoners did not by any means take over the government. Of the succession of Premiers until 1932,[3] only two were

---

[3] Hara (commoner), Takahashi (commoner), Kato (Admiral), Yamamoto (Admiral), Kiyoura (Peer), Kato (politician, but a

powerful figures, Hara and Hamaguchi, and they, together with the last, Inukai, were assassinated in office. With the exception of the Peer Kiyoura and the two Navy men Kato and Yamamoto, however, they were all leaders of the majority party at the time they became premier, and thus qualified as politicians in this sense, at least.

Theoretically, then, the politicians had come into power. If, actually, their leaders had consistently been commoners as was Hara, their principal power would have resided in the new responsibility the Diet had to feel for them, and something approaching a Western structure might have been under way. As it was, only two of the important premiers were commoners, and the others were not satisfied to take their chances with the Lower House alone, but arranged compromises with the other elements of the government. These compromises became increasingly difficult to fulfill and in the end caused the leaders' destruction.

PROSPECTS FOR PARTY SUCCESS

On the one hand, then, as *Kensei no Jodo* got under way, the time seemed propitious for a happy trial of liberalism. The support of the Diet, and hence of the Japanese people, had begun to appear more potent than the feelings of the army. The oligarchy was passing away; in 1922 Yamagata died, and in 1924, Matsukata. The only remaining *Genro*, Saionji, heartily favored party government. In key positions, such as Lord Keeper of the Privy Seal (*Naidaijin*) and Minister of the Imperial Household (*Kunai-*

diplomat and joined by marriage to the Mitsubishi interests), Kato, Wakatsuki (bureaucrat), Tanaka (General), Hamaguchi (commoner), Wakatsuki, Inukai (commoner).

daijin), served such men as Makino and Ikki, who were noted for their broad and liberal views.

But beneath the surface, all was not so well. The only really powerful commoner leaders, Hara and Hamaguchi, were to be assassinated. With the end of the oligarchy in view, moreover, the new generation in the Army High Command made it plain that they would contest the succession to power with the politicians. They were determined that their views on army expansion and patriotic indoctrination should prevail, while the Navy was equally insistent that the civilians should not thwart its programs for fleet expansion by international commitments. Finally, there was little or no improvement in the notorious corruption of Japanese party politics. The people, on whom alone the parties could depend to support their regime, continued to experience periodic waves of disgust at the parties, the Diet, and all for which these bodies stood. The period of "The Party Politicians in Power" was to witness at least the first phase of a struggle for the control of the Japanese government among its newly crystallized elements, of which the end is not yet in sight.

KENSEI NO JODO BEGINS, 1918

Entering upon its duties in the beginning of October 1918, Hara's *Seiyukai* Cabinet at once attacked the economic problems the Terauchi Government had bequeathed it. Takahashi Korekiyo, the Finance Minister, was a business wizard; and while the general situation remained fundamentally unsound, conditions were ameliorated at least to the extent that the Cabinet continued to survive. Iron scandals in Kyushu and land scandals in Kyoto added to the general confusion; but perhaps precisely because these scandals seemed to involve everyone, the Cabinet again managed to remain in office.

In late 1918 the labor situation was somewhat improved by wage increases; a portion of the World War industrial boom was being shared with the workers. After the Peace of Versailles, however, wide restlessness reappeared, and the number of labor strikes increased ominously. Reciprocally, there arose an almost equally numerous group of organizations for combating "dangerous thoughts."[4]

Meanwhile the prestige of both the Government and the Army suffered by the fiasco that the Siberian Expedition was proving. Repercussions of the stand taken by the Allies not only took the form of anti-foreign resentment, but caused much criticism of the Hara Government for inept handling of foreign affairs. Despite Hara's personal popularity, the Diet that met in January 1920 was so obstreperous that the House was dissolved before it had passed a budget. The Cabinet was forced, therefore, to take enormous liberties with the budget of the previous year with the fervent hope that the new Diet could be persuaded to approve.

General elections were held under the electoral law passed the previous year, which had decreased the size of election districts and increased the number of representatives in the Lower House of the Diet. Of the new total of 464, the *Seiyukai* received 281 seats, and the *Kenseikai* 109. The *Seiyukai* thus controlled

---

[4] Outstanding among these were the *Roninkai* in 1918, and the *Kyochokai* in 1919. Similar societies were organized from time to time during this entire period, and new ones spring up sporadically even now despite the close regimentation at the present time of the whole Japanese nation. Such groups as these differ from the "Black Ocean Society" mentioned earlier in this work. "Organized reactionary pressure groups" would be a better description for them than "secret societies."

a large absolute majority, but when the Diet met in June 1920, a bitter quarrel within the party prevented the anticipated exhibition of mutual confidence between a Premier and the Diet majority. Hara wanted the Siberian affair to be kept as small as possible; the army, which had more influence with the *Seiyukai* than with any other party, insisted that it was to be given a free hand.

PREMIER HARA IS ASSASSINATED, 1921

Matters continued indecisive into 1921, with Hara continuing to pit his personal determination against the army steamroller, which was rapidly running out of steam, when the first major setback to the political parties occurred. On November 24, Hara was assassinated; significantly, by a crazed railroad employee, bitter at the degeneration of the times. Takahashi at once became Premier, but he was a financier, not a politician. Without the controlling leadership of Hara the quarrel within the *Seiyukai* threatened to become an open break. Seeing no reason to hold responsibility for what he could not control, Takahashi resigned. The *Seiyukai* split, and lost its absolute majority in the Lower House.

No single party being strong enough to set up its own cabinet, Admiral Kato Tomosaburo was commanded to become premier, after consultation between Saionji and Kiyoura, president of the Privy Council since Yamagata's death a few months before. Kato had been Navy Minister in the last two Cabinets, so that he was assured of at least some *Seiyukai* support. After his death in office—from natural causes—in the late summer of 1923, he was succeeded by Admiral Count Yamamoto. These were nonparty cabinets, but they continued to lean more consistently on the *Seiyukai* than elsewhere, and such *Seiyukai* stalwarts as Inukai Ki and Inoue Junnosuke were included among their members.

The confusion that had plagued the highest offices of government since Hara's murder had penetrated even farther. The year 1921 was famous not only for its series of assassinations, attacks on liberal organizations, and meetings by organized bullies (*sōshi*), but also for the richest crop of scandals in a decade. Early in 1922, while Takahashi was premier, the Diet became irrepressible. Everything, from fist fights among members to the throwing of a live snake from the gallery upon the House floor, was offered to keep up flagging interest. More serious to the Government, there appeared a marked swing to the Left in popular thought. Such cries as "Soviets are better than Diets" were answered by the Cabinet through the introduction of a "dangerous thoughts suppression" bill; but the session ended before the bill reached a vote. *Sōshi* (hired bullies) were increasingly employed by every kind of organization, particularly to smash labor unions and ruin the offices and persons of overliberal newspapers and their editors.

THE EARTHQUAKE BRINGS A "TRANSCENDENT" CABINET, 1923

On September 1, 1923 the great Tokyo earthquake made a shambles of the Emperor's capital. The Yamamoto Cabinet, set up the following day, declared itself "transcendent," and police immediately arrested over a thousand residents of Tokyo, most of them socialists. Out of this came one incident which did not augur well for the development of liberal institutions in Japan. A captain of gendarmerie, one Amakasu, caused the arrest of the prominent labor leader Osugi Sakae together with his wife and seven-year-old nephew, and with his own hands strangled them. When the news finally became known, he was court-martialed and sentenced to ten years' imprisonment, although several of the more excitable newspapers called him a national hero. This was perhaps *wasn't he?* the first occasion on which a junior military officer, more or less successfully, undertook to guide the destinies of Japan by his own hands. *(N. B.)*

The transcendency of Yamamoto's Cabinet lifted the Government above all the parties equally; and this gave the parties their only possible opportunity to band together for a synchronized bombardment of the Premier. Both large parties wanted a share in the post-earthquake reconstruction, and if they were not given it, they were quite determined that no one else should obtain it either. Completely disgusted, Yamamoto seized upon the attempted assassination of the Prince Regent at the Diet meeting on December 27, 1923[5] to retire his Cabinet.

Two nonparty Cabinets in succession caused the major parties considerable anxiety, and immediately upon Yamamoto's resignation they instituted a series of conferences among themselves toward arranging a recovery of normalcy in government. Meanwhile, however, Viscount Kiyoura, president of the Privy Council, had been hurriedly interviewing the aged Matsukata and Saionji, and as well the Minister of the Imperial Household and the Lord Keeper of the Privy Seal. As one of His Majesty's principal advisers, Kiyoura then managed to persuade the Imperial Throne that the only man for the premiership

[5] The would-be assassin, who hoped by killing the Prince Regent to encourage much-needed reform, was finally hanged on November 15 of the following year.

was Viscount Kiyoura. He formed an extremely conservative cabinet at once, drawn entirely from the House of Peers.

At this the parties were outraged. They flatly refused to co-operate, and Kiyoura was forced to dissolve the House of Representatives on January 31, 1924. The parties waged a vituperative campaign for the ensuing elections. When a train in which some political leaders were traveling was wrecked, the Government was at once accused of choosing this particularly underhanded way of disposing of the opposition. On June 6 Kiyoura resigned, for in the elections the *Kenseikai* had won 146 seats, the *Seiyuhonto*[6] 120, and the *Seiyukai* 101—and all were banded against him.

PARTY GOVERNMENT IS RESUMED, 1924

Shortly afterward, Kato Takaakira, president of the *Kenseikai*, became Premier, with the support of a coalition including the *Kenseikai*, the *Seiyukai*, the *Kakushin* Club, and others. Under this Cabinet, a fairly liberal policy was possible, for as Foreign Minister in Okuma's 1915 Cabinet Kato had been responsible for the Twenty-one Demands, and therefore it was felt that his attitude toward China would be satisfactorily firm. Baron Shidehara's appointment as Foreign Minister caused widespread disgust, however, for he was known to favor a "conciliatory" policy toward China; few things could cause greater suspicion of a Cabinet than that.

Kato's Cabinet was frequently termed a Mitsubishi Government, for both he and Shidehara were

---

[6] After Hara's death and during Takahashi's premiership, the *Seiyukai* had split into two groups, one of which retained the name *Seiyukai*, while the other took the name *Seiyu-honto*.

related by marriage to the Iwasaki family. It was not long before the several party factions in the coalition began to quarrel and draw apart again. The weight of the Cabinet, including Kato, tended to the *Kenseikai*, which has been identified with the Mitsubishi interests, while the *Seiyukai* and its aggressive Mitsui connections found more and more fault with the Kato Government. Under "Lion" Hamaguchi (*Kenseikai*) the Finance Ministry was directing a strong movement toward economy and retrenchment in administration; this did not please either the more military group or the bureaucrats who were so prominent in the *Seiyukai*.

One major legislative accomplishment must be credited to this coalition group, and this was actually made possible by the fact of the coalition. Both major parties had coveted the honor of passing the Universal Manhood Suffrage bill, which enfranchised practically all males over twenty-five years of age; as a result, each party had prevented the other from doing anything about it. Now that they were in coalition, however, it became quite simple; and with a considerable fanfare the electorate was increased from three million to approximately thirteen million.

THE CAMPAIGN AGAINST "DANGEROUS THOUGHTS," 1925

Such liberalism as this did not exist without counterbalancing activities on the opposite side, however. Principally under the direction of the reactionary Minister of Education, Dr. Okada, a vigorous war was declared on "dangerous thoughts," particularly against students. Young men were arrested and held *incommunicado*; the study of socialism and such dangerous subjects was forbidden.[7] Finally, in April 1925, the famous Peace Preservation Law was passed. Under its provisions, those who formed or joined societies that had as an object the alteration of the national constitution or the form of government, or repudiation of the system of private ownership of property, would be subject to imprisonment for a term not exceeding ten years, with or without hard labor. Instigation of such ideas could be penalized by seven years' imprisonment. The Act was later amended to include the death penalty in certain cases. Home Minister Wakatsuki, who was later to fail in an attempt to stem the forces of a more purely militaristic reaction, now spoke earnestly in favor of the Act, the administration of which would come largely under the supervision of his Ministry. In the House of Peers, only Marquis Tokugawa opposed it. While it by no means caused the first political arrests in Japan, this Law did inaugurate the policy of mass incarcerations which have since its passage become rather familiar.

THE ARMY IS REORGANIZED

It was principally the elements whose love of liberalism was not deep, but who desired to have the Western nations regard Japan as a progressive, liberal state, who advertised widely at this time the "demilitarization" of the country. The postwar military reorganization plan, developed in the early twenties,

---

[7] At the present time University students are permitted, and sometimes required, to read a list of books in economics that includes the classics of communism; but they are only permitted to read such works after they have satisfied the academic authorities that their training and knowledge in economics according to the Japanese philosophy is sufficiently complete to enable them to criticize Marxian thought intelligently rather than succumb to it.

involved the reduction of the strength of the army both by divisions and by total peacetime man power. In March 1925 the major step was taken, with the disbandment of four recently organized divisions. After the unpleasant popular reaction to the Siberian Expedition, the military men were not dissatisfied to remain out of the public eye; their own partisans, therefore, were among the most vociferous in pointing out the increasingly pacific nature of the Japanese government.

In reality there was no cessation whatever of military activity. The officers from the disbanded divisions were not in general retired; they were assigned to the schools, where, approximately at the same time, a new system of military service was being organized. It was similar to—although more rigorous than—the American R.O.T.C. The seventeen-division army structure, which was left after the removal of four divisions, was considered by many prominent officers to suit the peacetime needs of the army better than the more bulky organization. The money which was saved, the additional officer corps that resulted, and the equipment which was released were all put to new and better use, particularly in developing the tactical lessons of the World War, such as tanks, machine guns, and airplanes; for since the war the Japanese army had lagged considerably behind the European forces in this respect. So far as the psychological aspects of militarism are concerned, while the nation could boast a smaller army, the percentage of subjects who were now exposed to some degree of military training and indoctrination, particularly through the schools, was greatly increased.

In August 1925 the quarrels between the *Kenseikai* and the *Seiyukai* factions in the coalition cabinet caused its end. Kato returned to the premiership immediately, with a new Government formed completely from the *Kenseikai* party (soon to become the *Minseito*), of which he was president. Baron Shidehara retained his post as Foreign Minister, and the Diet and the Army continued to attack his China policy. In December, upon the rebellion of a Chinese general from Chang Tso-lin, the Warlord of Manchuria, the exponents of a "positive policy" agitated that Japan should take action to preserve her interests in China. Shidehara refused to meddle in affairs he considered not his own. Unconcerned, the Japanese Railway Guard Troops in Manchuria moved in such a way that the rebellious general was trapped and killed. Chang was properly grateful, and at this the Army was satisfied. So far as the Foreign Minister and the civilians were concerned, it was another symptom of a chronic disease in the Japanese government which careful observers were already able to label "dual diplomacy."

SCANDALS DOMINATE POLITICS

Towards the end of December, Premier Kato died. Wakatsuki succeeded to the presidency of the *Kenseikai* and to the premiership, while "Lion" Hamaguchi replaced him as Home Minister. This Cabinet lasted until April 1927, but its career was not entirely pleasant. On the one hand, large and vociferous elements opposed its foreign policy, because Shidehara had remained as Foreign Minister. On the other hand, there was considerable dissatisfaction among the people; on December 1 a Farmer-Labor Party (*Nomin Rodoto*) had been permitted by the Government to organize, but, perhaps because it claimed 140,000 members, it was dispersed on the same day.

In order to drive the attacks from the forces of reaction and the forces of radicalism into the background, the *Kenseikai* supported its Government by a virulent attack on the *Seiyukai*. General Baron Tanaka, that party's new president, suffered the brunt of the campaign; first it was claimed that he was receiving bribes, and then he was accused of malversations of secret service funds in connection with the Siberian Expedition. Although these charges followed Tanaka until his death, none of them was ever proved. In turn, the Government was charged with lack of discipline and strictness. Silly trivia formed the basis for most of the heated Diet debates; terrific scandals were raised over nothing, simply to force the Government out of office. Premier Wakatsuki himself was accused in connection with certain unpleasant scandals. No better example than the Diet session of 1926 could be found to demonstrate the nonsense on which politics were now based, and the depths into which they had fallen.

Although it still held a majority in the House of Representatives, and had not been defeated on any important measure, the Wakatsuki Cabinet resigned on April 18, 1927. It had created great antagonism in less liberal quarters by its failure to adopt a more "positive" China policy, and this undoubtedly influenced the Privy Council in refusing its approval of the Cabinet's proposals in the financial problems revolving about the unhappy plight of the Bank of Taiwan (Formosa). The way was opened, therefore, for the *Seiyukai* to undertake at once to satisfy the more militarist and conservative groups, toward which it leaned on many matters of policy, and to assure the continuance of real party government.

TANAKA FORMS A SEIYUKAI CABINET, 1927

General Baron Tanaka Giichi, who had become head of the *Seiyukai* upon Takahashi's resignation a few years before, now formed a Cabinet in which Takahashi held the portfolio of Finance. At once the *Kenseikai* beat to new heights of foulness the scandal about Tanaka's alleged misuse of secret military funds on the Siberian Expedition. Nor did it hesitate, as it still controlled a majority, to carry through the House of Representatives a resolution impeaching the Privy Council for refusing to support Wakatsuki on the Bank of Taiwan affair. Actual resolutions of no confidence were only avoided by dissolution or proroguing when they seemed imminent.

Tanaka himself was high in the councils of the second generation of the Choshu clique, but with the exception of his War and Navy Ministers, his Cabinet was composed entirely of *Seiyukai* members. He retained the portfolio of Foreign Affairs, with the result that the storms aroused over his conduct of the government were concentrated mostly upon himself as an army leader, as head of the Cabinet, and as the Minister directly responsible for the unhappy developments in foreign relations. Eventually large sections of his own *Seiyukai* felt free to criticize him. At the outset of his Ministry, the *Seiyukai* was in the minority in the House of Representatives.

In order to prevent a vote of no confidence, Tanaka dissolved the Diet shortly after it had assembled for the regular 1927-28 session. Despite liberal expenditures of money by his party, the Premier found after the elections that no substantial change in alignment had taken place. Dr. Suzuki Kisaburo retired as Home Minister after the campaign; it was the second

time since the promulgation of the Constitution that
the Government had lost an election. With this Diet,
1928-29 was an even more turbulent year. A short
special session late in 1928 had to be suspended twice
to prevent the passage of no confidence resolutions.
The regular session in 1928-29 was unmitigated misery for Baron Tanaka; although his Cabinet managed to weather the attacks of the Diet, it was forced
to resign—to the relief of all—shortly after the ad-
journment.

Two principal problems—relations with China and
the Pact of Paris—continued to trouble this Ministry
throughout its career. An analysis of these problems
best shows the relations of the different organs of
government with each other at this stage, and most
correctly presages the trend of future events.

A "POSITIVE CHINA POLICY"

Chang Tso-lin, the Warlord of Manchuria, was
friendly to Japanese influence; but by the summer of
1927 the southern expeditionary forces under Chiang
Kai-shek had made such progress that it began to
appear probable that a contest for power in northern
China, displeasing to Japan, was due in the near future. It was not long before the activities of the Japanese Kwantung Army in Shantung occasioned a protest from the Chinese Nationalist Government; and
by April 1928 matters had become serious.[8] During
May 1928, Japanese troops were sent to China, osten-
sibly to protect Japanese lives and property in the
face of the Nationalist Army's northern advance.
These troops, however, took the attitude that they

[8] For a careful discussion of Sino-Japanese problems of the
Tanaka Government, see chapters "The Tsinan Incident" and
"A Grave Manchurian Incident" in Takeuchi, *op. cit.*, pp. 247-261
and 275-282.

were to check that advance—depending on the friendship of Chang Tso-lin—for reasons of policy, and to demonstrate the reality of Premier Tanaka's somewhat vaguely stated "positive policy" toward China. The whole affair was managed by the military command working with Tanaka, but with remarkably little reference to the civilian authorities; indeed, officers on the spot acted with an embarrassing independence of the War Ministry.

In the current Diet session, the *Minseito* (the old *Kenseikai*) accused Tanaka of using the Tsinan Incident merely for domestic policy; the general debate was unpleasant, but fortunately for Tanaka the Diet adjourned on May 6, when the incident had just begun. As things became worse at Tsinan, however, more groups at home became worried, and still more became enraged. On June 4 Chang Tso-lin was killed by a bomb, under circumstances described in some quarters as criminal negligence on the part of the Japanese Army Railway Guard, and things looked critical. The authorities then determined to withdraw the troops slowly from the mainland. As the new Diet session approached, Tanaka and the Army grew more perturbed, for by December 1928 a large group in the House of Peers did not hesitate to voice its worry over Tanaka's China policy. In January 1929 the Diet convened again and made itself completely obnoxious to the Cabinet. Tanaka finally entered into negotiations with the Chinese Government to liquidate the Tsinan Incident, but dragged these out until just after the Diet had adjourned in the spring in order to save himself from the criticism he knew he would receive. Final settlement was reached at the end of March; but it was kept in the form of an executive agreement instead of a formal treaty, in order

to keep it from the scrutiny of the Privy Council—
which made that body furious. Here, then, was one
incident, on the final resolution of which no two of
the several governmental organs could manage to
agree.

THE PACT OF PARIS, 1928

The other matter which caused the Tanaka Government so much grief was the Pact of Paris. In July
1928 the Japanese plenipotentiaries agreed to sign
the treaty, after the arrangement of a condition
whereby the phrase "in the names of their respective
peoples" might, in the case of Japan, be interpreted
"on behalf of the people," since the Emperor was the
sole repository of sovereignty. By August the *Minseito* had become completely aroused on this point;
presently their wrath was approved by several influential Privy Councillors.[9] When the Diet met in January 1929 the Government found itself attacked on
both sides for the phraseology of the Pact: the liberals were enraged, and the conservatives wailed that
it imperiled the future of the country. The quarreling
continued long after the Diet session. After violent
debates, the Privy Council recommended ratification
with an attached statement that "in the names of
their respective peoples" did not apply to Japan. Foreign Minister Uchida was so upset by this reservation
that he resigned.

The Tanaka Cabinet was completely weary. So
far as the Diet was concerned, everything it did
was wrong. The death of Chang Tso-lin was a subject for heated discussion in the 1929 session; be-

[9] For an analysis of the consideration of the Pact of Paris by
the various organs of Japanese Government, see chapter "The
Pact of Paris" in Takeuchi, *op. cit.*, pp. 262-274.

cause Tanaka had begged that the matter should
not be brought up, he was attacked for trying to
stifle freedom of speech. His Foreign Minister had
resigned over ratification of the Peace Treaty. And
curses were still coming in from all sides about the
Manchurian affair. On July 2, 1929, therefore, the
Tanaka Cabinet resigned, and the *Minseito* returned
to power. Tanaka died at the end of the year, a poor
and broken man.

A MINSEITO CABINET UNDER HAMAGUCHI, 1929

"Lion" Hamaguchi had replaced Baron Wakatsuki as president of the *Minseito* after the latter's
Cabinet fell in 1927, and he now organized a *Minseito* Party Cabinet. Its foreign policy was unre-
servedly Shidehara's; the unsuccessful application
of a "positive policy" had provoked a natural popular reaction, and there was not much doubt that
Shidehara and Hamaguchi were as sincerely patriotic as Tanaka had been. The return of the *Minseito*,
moreover, meant a return to predominance of the
Mitsubishi type of interest—after all, Shidehara was
related to the family—which fitted in somewhat better with European concepts of world capitalism than
did the colonial and self-sufficient interest of the
Seiyukai's Mitsui backers. In world affairs, the Cabinet succeeded in putting through the London Naval
Limitation Treaty, although only at the cost of a
heated bout in which it was hinted that the Privy
Council might be packed if necessary. In Chinese affairs, a definitely "conciliatory" policy was pursued.[10]

[10] "Conciliatory" here has a doubly real sense, in that after the
recent incidents, China demanded a great deal of conciliation from
Japan if anything constructive was to be accomplished. Ordinarily,
however, the two terms, "positive" and "conciliatory," as applied
to Japanese policy toward China, represent the opposite means to

Diplomats who would be regarded with favor in Nanking were substituted for the domineering fire-eaters who had so antagonized the Nationalist Government before. Until diplomacy was taken from the Foreign Ministry's hands in the fall of 1931, much was accomplished by this policy toward the peaceable settlement of the numerous points at issue between the two governments. In domestic policy, Hamaguchi pressed more zealously than ever his determination for retrenchment and reform. By the reorganization of governmental administration, including the army, he aimed to reduce the running expenses of government, and to maintain an energetic fight against the world-wide depression, which Japan was only then beginning to feel. Then, in January 1930, under the full impact of the world financial crisis, the Cabinet took the additional step of putting a ban on gold exports.

In consequence of all this, while the Cabinet enjoyed the favor of a large section of the people—the liberals and certain classes of business magnates—it was cordially hated by others. Particularly, it

---

the same and advocated by the two major political factions of Japan. The *Seiyukai*, which has more consistently worked with at least the older leaders of the militarist group, has generally been identified with the "positive" policy. This may be partly explained by its close connection with the Mitsui interests. The Mitsui, while engaging in almost every form of capitalistic activity, has generally supported policies of cheap money and a colonial, mercantilist national economy. This works in well with the army's program for rigid Japanese control of a northern China which will become at once a source of raw supplies for Japanese industry and an open market for Japanese development.

The *Minseito* has been most closely affiliated with the Mitsubishi interests. The Mitsubishi, although perhaps the outstanding organization in Japanese heavy industry, are more interested in a broad horizontal commerce than in a vertical, all-encompassing and self-reciprocating Japanese industrial machine. They have favored sound money, and supported Hamaguchi's efforts to reform administration as one way to secure this.

incurred the resentment of the army, and of the newly crystallizing young militarist clique. The *Minseito* continued to hold its majority in the House of Representatives despite increasing *Seiyukai* opposition. The House of Peers, however, became increasingly unfavorable toward it; and the way in which the Cabinet was able to force through the London Naval Treaty convinced the conservatives and army supporters that only by quick and decisive action could they avoid the ruin of their ambitions and plans.

HAMAGUCHI IS ASSASSINATED, 1930

For the second and deciding time, party government received a crucial blow, when in November 1930, "Lion" Hamaguchi was shot by a fanatical youth. He did not die until April 1931, but he was unable to perform his duties; Shidehara served as Premier *ad interim*, and then Wakatsuki, and when Hamaguchi finally died Wakatsuki once again became president of the *Minseito* and Premier.

The Cabinet and its aims lost greatly by Hamaguchi's assassination. Above all, the strong leader, the politician who could hold the other politicians together, was gone. Shidehara lost much ground by his headship; he was a bureaucrat, and as the *Minseito* felt it owed him no allegiance, it attacked him as much as did the *Seiyukai*. Wakatsuki was well intentioned and somewhat more in touch with party politics; but he was in action, if not in ideas, irresolute. Compromise was his method, and he finished by compromising the liberals right out of power.

Under Wakatsuki the Cabinet continued Hamaguchi's program of "Retrenchment and Reform."

But it had only been the "Lion's" iron will and resolve that had pushed things along; this Wakatsuki
lacked. As a result, not only did the militarist clique
feel that something had to be done—now it felt that
something could be done.

It found its opportunity in the Mukden Incident
of September 18, 1931. This ended a four-month
struggle between the army, represented chiefly by
War Minister General Minami, and the Foreign Office headed by Baron Shidehara, over the method
to be followed in liquidating certain problems at
issue between the Japanese and Chinese governments. The army ended this struggle by ignoring the
Foreign Office; successful in this, they continued
largely to ignore the Foreign Office from that time
forward. The major activity of the Foreign Office
hence became justifying the *faits accomplis* of the
army, and presenting them in the most palatable
form possible to the outside world.

Wakatsuki's Cabinet found itself unable to
weather the storm the Manchuria Affair had aroused.
A split in the *Minseito* was the last straw. Home
Minister Adachi Kenzo, eager for the premiership,
proposed an emergency coalition cabinet with the
Seiyukai. When the Cabinet refused to consider this,
he refused to attend its meetings. Although he was
hand in glove with the military clique and the
Mitsui, and had from the first been cold to the retrenchment activities of Finance Minister Inoue
Junnosuke—son-in-law of Baron Iwasaki, head of
the Mitsubishi interests—Adachi's power in the
Minseito was such that it was impossible to eject
him from the Cabinet. On December 11, 1931 the
last *Minseito* Government resigned, and the *Seiyukai*
was given a final opportunity to demonstrate that

a party government could still cope with the situation.

THE SEIYUKAI FAILS TO CURB THE MILITARISTS, 1932

Inukai Ki, a professional politician who had succeeded Baron Tanaka in 1929 as president of the *Seiyukai*, now formed a Cabinet. It was still a party rather than a coalition Government; Adachi was not included, for after all, he was officially a *Minseito* member. In January the Diet was dissolved, the Government winning the elections by a landslide which replaced the *Minseito* majority by an alignment of 304 *Seiyukai* seats against 147 *Minseito*.

At once, the Cabinet attempted to apply *Seiyukai* ideas of a more positive China policy, but they quickly learned that affairs of China policy had been withdrawn quite definitely from the hands of the politicians. They were unable, moreover, to cope with the internal crisis in Japan that had been aroused by a combination of economic conditions, social unrest, the army's efforts to control policy, and the continuation of the Manchurian adventure —with all its implications, including Western displeasure, the action of the League of Nations, and the decisive Japanese reaction thereto.

On January 8, 1932 a bomb was thrown at an Imperial Procession; the Inukai Cabinet assumed responsibility and presented its resignation, but received an Imperial Command to continue in office. The following month, Inoue Junnosuke, former Minister of Finance, was assassinated; then in March, Baron Dan, Manager of the Mitsui interests which were largely backing the *Seiyukai*, was killed. The internal situation was running rapidly beyond any ability the political parties could show to control it.

The crisis came on May 15, 1932 when a group of young military and naval officers terrorized Tokyo for several hours, attacking banks, the Metropolitan Police Headquarters, and the headquarters of the *Seiyukai*. Premier Inukai himself was assassinated. Minister of Finance Takahashi assumed the premiership, and Dr. Suzuki Kisaburo, an influential member of the *Seiyukai*, took over the party leadership. But an era had ended. Prince Saionji, the aged *Genro*, was on his way to Tokyo to consult with the Emperor on the selection of a new Premier. The political activities of the conservative and militarist elements in the government and the nation had emasculated the civil authority; now, under personal attacks and the rise of popular agitation, the power of the politicians was broken.

CHAPTER VII

THE MILITARISTS IN POWER (1932–1945)

DURING the "struggle for power"[1] which had engaged the factions in the Japanese Government since the Tanaka regime, the West had observed developments in Japan with keen interest. It was at this time that the struggle between fascism and democracy in Europe was taking concrete form, and occidental commentators made much of resemblances to this struggle in the Japanese scene. One vital factor was generally ignored, however, and interpretations which ignored it were therefore fundamentally wrong. That factor was the principle of *Kodo*, the Imperial Way.

It was widely postulated, in the Occident, that the Japanese Diet was similar to the British Parliament; that the Japanese Cabinet was similar to the British Cabinet; that, in the large, the government of Japan at the beginning of the Hamaguchi Cabinet was similar to what were called the demo-

[1] Naturally a tremendous amount of literature on this "struggle for power" has appeared in Western languages. Much of it is careful and useful; but the greatest general failing is a tendency to view these Japanese developments as if they were taking place in a European *milieu*. The present account is based principally on Japanese sources. Students who wish to go deeper into these recent problems may profit by reading, in addition to the back files of such newspapers as the *New York Times*, these works: T. A. Bisson, *Japan in China* (New York, 1938); E. and E. Lederer, *Japan in Transition* (New Haven, 1938); O. Tanin and E. Yohan, *Militarism and Fascism in Japan* (New York, 1934); R. K. Reischauer, "Conflicts Inside Japan," *Harpers Magazine* (July, 1936); R. K. Reischauer, "The Disunity of the Japanese Militarists," *Amerasia* Magazine (March, 1937). [J. R.]

cratic governments in Europe. It was recognized that
the army, and army men, had a perhaps unusual
influence upon the civil government; but it was
certainly not said that Imperial, Constitutional
Japan was to be classed with Italy, then the prime
example of the Fascist State.

As the army men, by now widely termed "militarists," took matters more into their own hands;
as the civil government's reluctance to follow the
"strong policy" of the militarists led to increasing
evidences of "dual diplomacy"; and as the civil government was gradually reduced to the role of apolo-
gist for the army's *faits accomplis*; Western observers
took a quick look at Europe, with its rising Nazi
Germany, and announced that in Japan too, fascism
was rising like a strong tide.

Fascism, however, was not rising in Japan, and
despite the existence of active fascist movements,
the characteristics of what political theory calls fascism are not prominent in the Japanese Government today. Japan was then becoming, and now
largely is, it is true, a totalitarian state; but so is
Soviet Russia. The principle of totalitarianism in
Japan is not the dictatorship of the national genius,
as in fascism, nor the dictatorship of the proletariat,
as in communism; it is the dictatorship of the divine
state which is embodied in the Japanese Emperor
and follows the Imperial Way. The instrument of
that dictatorship is the military class, which, tradi-
tionally independent of the Emperor's civil advisers,
has decided that the principle of the Imperial Way
cannot be followed or maintained by the kind of
government which those civil advisers have directed
during the last twenty years.

Not everyone in Japan agrees with the military

class that the Imperial Way can be followed best by a dictatorship of the military class. Since they discredited the politicians, and assumed a more direct control of the government, the military group itself has several times been discredited, and not least by serious divisions within its own ranks. They have had several times to retire from the foreground of public attention, and use the bureaucrats for a front. The nature of their peculiar position in the Japanese body politic, however, has kept for them the deciding power over how the Japanese Government shall appear and what it shall do. From the end of the World War until 1931, they exercised this power under the surface, and in the face of an ever-increasing opposition from powerful civilian leaders such as Hamaguchi. By 1932, however, the politicians obviously had lost all ability to control the course of events. The military group then had no choice but to take their place, and prove the validity of the command they had won.

GOVERNMENT UNDER MILITARIST DOMINATION BEGINS, 1932

Certain Japanese personalities had become prominent because of the popular personification in them of the military power. Of these, none outshines General Araki Sadao, the brilliant, ascetic son of a poor family from the agrarian districts about Tokyo. Of enormous influence with the younger officers of the army, he had been chosen by the High Command for the post of War Minister in the *Seiyukai* Cabinet which Inukai had formed at the close of 1931. He was to act as the military's watchdog in the last chance that they were giving party government to make good.

Immediately after Inukai's assassination in the May 15 Incident of 1932, the *Seiyukai* leaders, who had hastily elected Dr. Suzuki their president, came to an agreement with Araki for continuation of a *Seiyukai* Cabinet. Less partisan but more intelligently liberal elements, however, saw only disaster in the continuation of this inevitably dual form of government. Saionji particularly, therefore, advised the establishment of a "National Cabinet," led by a nonparty man but including politicians, as a safer compromise between the parliamentarians and what was already being called fascism. On May 26, therefore, a Cabinet was formed by Admiral Saito, made up of five party members,[2] three members of the House of Peers, two bureaucrats, and three militarists.[3] The Cabinet was carefully chosen. Admiral Saito was a "militarist," but came from the navy, not the army, and moreover, was retired. He was certainly not a party man, but he did not share in the army's bitter detestation of the parties. Further, General Araki's excitability in the War Office was balanced by Admiral Okada's calm diplomacy in the Navy Ministry. Inclusion of party members at a time when it was evident that the whole party system might not live much longer, forced the *Minseito* and *Seiyukai* to support the cabinet in self-protection; any crisis might be blamed on them or their representatives in the Government.

INTERNAL FRICTIONS TROUBLE THE PARTIES

As 1932 wore on, however, this compromise proved no freer than any earlier ones from the active con-

---

[2] Three from *Seiyukai*, two from *Minseito*.

[3] Premier Admiral Saito, Navy Minister Admiral Okada, War Minister General Araki.

flicts. Both *Seiyukai* and *Minseito* members, it is true, introduced a bill to recognize the new army-created state of Manchoukuo. This the Diet passed unanimously. The major parties nonetheless continued to suffer division within themselves, which made co-operation more and more difficult between the liberal party elements and those outside the parties who favored parliamentary government. Continuing his break with the *Minseito*, former Home Minister Adachi, after several other attempts, finally organized the *Kokumin Domei* (National Union Party), with the full status of a political party; and rallied under his leadership some thirty-two Diet members mostly recruited from the *Minseito*. In its program, the *Kokumin Domei* specifically and definitely favored fascism.

The *Seiyukai*, on the other hand, retained its party organization, but at the expense of party unity on matters of policy. After several breaks, the group which opposed co-operation with nonparty cabinets prevailed; those who accepted portfolios in such cabinets were formally read out of the party.

At the same time that the major parties were suffering internal dissensions, the *Shakai Minshuto* (Social Democrats) and *Zenkoku-Rono-Taishuto* (Farmer Labor Party) joined to form the *Shakai Taishuto* (People's Socialist Party). It had no particularly revolutionary significance, yet as it was the one mass party permitted to continue more or less unmolested by the authorities, its appearance carried a certain importance.

On September 5, 1932 the sixty-third Diet adjourned. It had approved the supplementary budget and it had passed numerous measures in an effort to cope with the depression. Again, apart from more

purely political activities, the next Diet, which ended
on March 25, 1933, followed its predecessor in passing economic legislation. The year 1933, however,
witnessed a revival of tenseness in public affairs.
General Araki's invention of the "crisis of 1935-
1936" effectively focused attention on the "foreign
menace";[4] and as a result, the army and navy were
successful in their demands for the larger part of
the 1934 budget. Araki proposed, however, a reform
of the tax system which would shift the weight of
the burden from the agrarian classes to those of
finance and industry. Failure to persuade the rest
of the Cabinet to endorse this proposal and several
farm relief measures, was a major factor in causing
his resignation as War Minister in 1934. His demands that so much money should be expended
merely for the relief of agrarian distress incurred
the resentment of a large part of the Army Command. His influence, or perhaps his usefulness, did
not decline, however, among the young officers,
many of whom came from the same sort of poor
agrarian background as he.

By April 1933 the leaders of the *Seiyukai* had
definitely decided to withdraw their support from
the Saito Cabinet. The budget had been passed, tremendous as it was, because in a state of emergency
everyone had worked together. The *Seiyukai*, however, had 290 seats to the *Minseito's* 110, and it had
expected that at the end of the Diet session a
Seiyukai Cabinet would return to power under the

[4] General Araki's "Crisis of 1935-1936" had particular reference
to the United States of America. In those years, according to his
thesis, the problems that America was causing for Japan would
come to an issue; and the Japanese people would have to steel
themselves for heroic sacrifice once and for all to rid the Far East
of this monster of the Pacific. For a good summary, see K. C.
Colegrove, *Militarism in Japan*. (Boston, 1936), pp. 48-51.

premiership of party president Suzuki. When Saito showed no signs of giving up the premiership the *Seiyukai* attempted to end his Cabinet by causing his Finance Minister, the venerable Takahashi, to resign. At the request of Saito and Prince Saionji, Takahashi refused to be his party's tool. Suzuki was offered a ministership without portfolio, but enraged by these proceedings, he refused it. At that point, there was an unofficial split within the *Seiyukai* between those who favored supporting the "national coalition" and those who would have nothing to do with it. For the moment Suzuki decided to take no action, but the following year the party definitely declared its opposition to the Cabinet.

Meanwhile differences among the War, Navy, Foreign, and Finance Ministers had caused the creation of a "Cabinet Conference Council" which, at the end of October 1933 had determined upon the policy for the budget to be submitted to the Diet. The appointment of a "liberal militarist" seemed in this sense at least to be improving co-operation among the government factions.

LIBERALISM AND REACTION IN DELICATE BALANCE

During 1934 it was doubtful whether liberalism or reaction was on the wane. On the one hand, contrary to all precedent, Baron Hiranuma, Vice-President of the Privy Council, was passed over in the appointment to that Council's presidency in May. Baron Ikki Kitokuro assumed that position on the nomination of Prince Saionji; Ikki was a liberal, and it was commonly said that the *Genro* disapproved of Hiranuma's close connection with the reactionary *Kokuhonsha* (Nationalist Society). It was generally rumored that Saionji was anxious to see liberals ap-

pointed as Lord Keeper of the Privy Seal, Minister
of the Imperial Household, and President of the
Privy Council, because he expected these officials
to take over the duties of Elder Statesmen when
he died.

On the other hand, the Army was vigilant lest
any statements, far less activities, should prejudice
the purity of the Japanese spirit; and in this it found
excellent deputies in large factions of the House of
Peers, the bureaucracy, the ex-service men's and
other patriotic societies, and even in the parties.
Baron Nakashima, Saito's Minister of Commerce,
was compelled to resign when it was discovered that
in an article written ten years previously, he had
compared the *Shogun* Ashikaga Takauji, who had
subdued the Emperor Go-Daigo in 1335, to Oliver
Cromwell.

Not satisfied with what had already been done
to endanger parliamentary government, a faction of
the *Seiyukai* made itself equally obnoxious to the
Cabinet and to the rest of its own party during the
Diet session in the winter of 1934. It was said by
some, however, that it was a fascist group which
was attempting thus to destroy the *Seiyukai*. In any
case, the Government lost several of its members by
resignation because of scandals that were aired, and
when the session ended, Saito himself was only kept
from resigning by Saionji's request. The search for
scandals finally bore fruit. The finance department
was so deeply involved that on July 1, the whole
Cabinet resigned.

ADMIRAL OKADA CONTINUES THE COMPROMISE, 1934

The *Minseito* had too few Diet seats to be able
to form a Ministry, and a serious split prevented the

Seiyukai from taking any concerted action. Saionji recommended Admiral Okada for the premiership after a joint conference with all the living ex-Premiers, the President of the Privy Council, and the Lord Keeper of the Privy Seal. The *Genro* desired a continuation of the arrangement that had obtained under Saito. In an attempt to secure a "national" character for the Cabinet, he approached Suzuki and Wakatsuki, presidents of the *Seiyukai* and *Minseito* respectively. Suzuki refused any official party support of the new Cabinet, and the three *Seiyukai* members who accepted portfolios were ejected from the party. Wakatsuki, on the other hand, was co-operative and supported his two members who retained their old posts under the new Cabinet. One result of this was the practical abandonment of attempts for *Seiyukai-Minseito* co-operation, for now the *Minseito* was more or less behind the Cabinet, while the *Seiyukai* at least tacitly opposed it.

War Minister Hayashi, Navy Minister Osumi, and Foreign Minister Hirota also agreed to stand at their posts under the new Premier; thus with a Cabinet including seven bureaucrats and militarists, and five party men, Okada took over the Government. A further compliment to the parties came when the new Cabinet chose for the twenty-four Parliamentary Vice-Minister and Counsellorships, nine *Seiyukai*, nine *Minseito*, and six members of the House of Peers.

In the fall of 1934 a new furor was created by the army's publication of the first of a series of pamphlets on patriotism and national defense.[5] A few days after

[5] As complete as anything that has appeared in English on these army pamphlets is Kenneth C. Colegrove, *Militarism in Japan* (Boston, 1936).

its appearance, War Minister Hayashi was constrained to assure the Cabinet and Diet that the army had no intention of acting on the rather disturbing social and economic policies brought forth in the pamphlets. Their aim, he declared, was solely public enlightenment.

Meanwhile, home government was inevitably affected, and relations between it and army elements were increasingly disturbed by the reorganization of the administration of the government and economics of Manchuria. The Manchurian Affairs Board was created under the control of the Premier and two days later War Minister General Hayashi was appointed President of the Manchurian Bureau. Decentralization of Manchurian control despite such efforts remained a problem. There was a strong tendency in the face of this toward an automatic concentration of control in the military officer who, by custom, was appointed at once Ambassador to Manchoukuo, Commander of Japanese forces on the mainland, and Governor of Kwantung Leased Territory.

THE "NATIONAL POLITY" FUROR, 1935

Attacks on liberals and liberal ideas grew more furious than ever in 1935, and beset as it was with continuing economic and social problems, the Cabinet had, nevertheless, to give much of its attention to the "national polity" issue which was so upsetting the nation. Dr. Minobe Tatsukichi was attacked early in the year because lectures and books which he had written as Professor of Constitutional Law at Tokyo University advanced the theory that the Emperor was only an organ of the State. Although Minobe was now a member of the House of Peers, Premier Okada and Home Minister Goto refused to suppress the book in question. At first there was little excitement over the books; then a formal complaint of *lese majesty* was filed by a Diet member, and from that point until the end of the year few issues surpassed this in the attention of the nation.

War Minister Hayashi announced to the press that the issue involved national thought, and must certainly be dealt with. The following week the House of Representatives passed a unanimous resolution drafted by the major parties in conjunction, asking the government to clarify the form of the national polity. Despite other new and difficult problems, the debate continued over the summer. In September, Dr. Minobe resigned from the House of Peers, and the pressure against him and others who had become involved in the general investigation of belief on national polity, was somewhat relieved. The issue did not die by any means, however; the *Seiyukai*, which had outrivaled the militarists in explosive indignation during the whole "crisis," heartily approved of their "National Polity Clarification Committee's" dissatisfaction with Premier Okada's attitude on the question. At the Cabinet session on September 20, Minobe's theory received principal attention, and the War and Navy Ministers declared their strong dissatisfaction. On October 15 the Cabinet finally issued a new joint statement on national polity, in which it stated that the Constitution rested on the principle that sovereignty resided in the Emperor; and that any idea of the State as a repository of sovereignty could not be abided.

BUREAUCRACY GAINS A STRONGER FOOTHOLD

Meanwhile changes had occurred in both the civilian and the military organs of government. The bureaucracy gained a stronger foothold in the civilian government by the establishment on May 11, 1935 of the *Naikaku Shigikai* (Cabinet Inquiry Council). Its fifteen members included four veteran statesmen, four members of the House of Peers, five members of the House of Representatives, and two financial leaders. Its completely national basis was prejudiced by the refusal of the *Seiyukai* to co-operate. But the bureaucrats, by whom principally its recommendations were to be prepared, hailed its creation as a move to stabilize the government.

Its first duty, however, was not a very encouraging one. The Government requested it to discover how to balance the national budget by improving the financial conditions of national and prefectural governments. There were no important militarists on the Council, and it might have been possible to achieve unity on a proposal to balance the budget by reducing armaments. Any tampering with the army appropriations by a nonarmy group, however, would have produced a violent reaction among the military; the only pathway toward real accomplishment open to the Council, therefore, was at the same time a pathway toward its own inevitable damnation.

UNREST WITHIN THE ARMY

In July 1935 a radical rearrangement of the Army High Command, also reaching deep into the ranks, became known. It was directed by War Minister General Hayashi and Prince Kan'in Kotohito, the Chief of the General Staff.[6]

Beginning with General Mazaki Jinzaburo, In-

[6] By this time Imperial Princes headed both General Staffs; Prince Kan'in the Army, and Prince Higashi-Fushimi the Navy.

spector General of Military Education, some thirty-five hundred changes of command were decreed and approved by the Emperor in order to create greater "army unity." A secretly circulated pamphlet asserted that this purge was really instigated by General Nagata, Director of the Military Affairs Bureau of the War Ministry, in an attempt to supplant the Araki-Mazaki faction with the Ugaki group.[7] Before all the changes had been effected, General Nagata was murdered in his office by one of the young officers, Lieutenant-Colonel Aizawa. Field-Marshal Prince Kan'in, General Hayashi, and General Watanabe, the "Big Three" of the Army, were agreed that there was need for stricter discipline in the army. The younger officers were offering too real a challenge to their superiors, and military efficiency could not be maintained if politics divided the army. Taking responsibility for the assassination, War Minister Hayashi resigned. But General Kawashima Yoshiyuki who succeeded him, took no further steps in the attempt, if it was one, to break up the Araki-Mazaki clique. The Army issued a statement, regretting remarks to the effect that a national emergency had been caused by it, and maintained that its program must have the support of the whole nation.

"FASCISM" BECOMES A CAMPAIGN ISSUE, 1936

On January 21, 1936 the Diet convened. The *Seiyukai* resolved to use its majority to pass a vote of

[7] Araki and Mazaki are the principal representatives of the "Young Officers." They are leaders of, and spokesmen for, the new officer group which has been striving to replace the clan cliques in the army; they advocate not only a strong foreign policy, but definite reform in the Japanese social system. Ugaki, if not truly liberal, has at least been more favorable to the older cliques of capitalists and politicians.

no confidence in the Ministry; it still raised the national polity issue, it wanted a party Cabinet, and it attacked the lack of harmony between defense and industry. The Government announced that the nature of the Diet debates was preventing just such harmony, and dissolved the House. Premier Okada and Finance Minister Takahashi took the unprecedented step of addressing a Government-sponsored mass meeting during the ensuing election campaign. The wide public interest evoked was expressed in the voting; 11,100,000 votes were cast, representing some eighty per cent of the electorate. The returns demonstrated the change in popular opinion; the *Seiyukai* lost its Diet majority to the *Minseito*. The *Minseito* slogan had been: "Which shall it be—parliamentary government or fascism?" while the *Seiyukai* urged the voters, "Down with the spurious coalition Government." In the end, even President Suzuki of the *Seiyukai* lost his Diet seat, which was unprecedented.

Final election returns showing that the Okada Government would have a wide support in the new Diet, were made known on February 22, 1936. On the morning of February 26, the third regiment of the First Division—stationed in Tokyo en route for Manchuria, and composed of one thousand men supplied with ammunition—followed twenty junior officers in an attempted overthrow of the Government. They killed Finance Minister Takahashi, Keeper of the Privy Seal Admiral Saito, and Inspector of Military Education General Watanabe; they thought they had killed Premier Okada. Many others were wounded. The entire regiment barricaded themselves in the streets of Tokyo. This was not the first time that army men had taken matters into their own hands, and certainly not the first plot to assassinate authorities. Several such plots had been uncovered during Saito's premiership, and one of some significance as early as October of 1931. This was the first, however, which was so extensive; the first which used common soldiers; and when an Imperial Command to disperse was ignored, this was the first to commit what was unquestionably the most serious kind of mutiny.

EFFECTS OF THE FEBRUARY 1936 ARMY MUTINY

So far as the people of Tokyo were concerned, the affair was liquidated in a few weeks. Its repercussions, however, were felt for a long time. Naturally, the army's prestige had suffered an enormous blow. To demonstrate its profound humiliation, the seven generals on the Supreme War Council resigned, and of these Generals Araki, Mazaki, Hayashi, and Abe were retired, while the other three received different appointments. General Terauchi Juichi replaced the Minister of War; the command of the Kwantung Army—which went with the Ambassadorship to Manchoukuo—was shifted; General Minami, who gave up the post, became a Supreme War Councillor; and the commander of the Tokyo Garrison was replaced.

These changes were insignificant, however, compared with the loss to the nation by Takahashi's death. Since December 1931 the War and Navy Ministers had been forced to submit their budget demands to Finance Minister Takahashi. His position had enabled him not only to exercise some control over the militarist activities, but as the representative of the financial world in the Government, also to strengthen his official control by informing the militarists just how far the capitalists, of whom they could not be independent, would go with them. By his death the Government, the capitalists, and the peace of the nation all suffered equally.

The army, moreover, was not greatly injured by its loss of prestige. Apologists came forth at once, and pointed out that selfish quarreling among political parties, and lack of self-denial and sacrifice for the nation, were what brought about the uprising; if something were not done at once to purify the national spirit, there could be no guarantee against a recurrence. They insisted that the young captains and lieutenants involved were of poor agrarian families, striking back at the oppressors of their class. It appeared later in the semiofficial *Japan Times*, however, that among fourteen of the leaders, four were the sons of generals, one the son of a rear admiral, one the son of a colonel, and the other two the sons, respectively, of a lieutenant and a sergeant-major. Of the rest, only one was the son of a farmer, although one, the son of a town headsman, probably came from a well-to-do agrarian family.

No event in recent Japanese history better demonstrates the complexity of the conflicts inside the nation than do these assassinations. Among those who were killed was General Watanabe Jotaro, Inspector-General of Military Education. Why should he have been killed? For the same reason that General Nagata had been assassinated. These two soldiers believed literally in the Meiji Emperor's admonition to soldiers to avoid political matters. They represented a faction in the Japanese Army which also included Generals Ugaki Kazushige, Terauchi Juichi, and Abe Nobuyuki. Their high positions enabled them to enforce their views. As a result, the other group, of which the *Kokoku Seinen Shoko Domei* (Young Officers League) was the most explosive exponent, and which looked to Generals Araki and Mazaki for leadership, caused their assassination.[8]

THE BUREAUCRATS FORM A GOVERNMENT, 1936

On March 9, 1936 Hirota Koki formed a Cabinet. Although it included several party members, it brought the bureaucratic group, from which Hirota himself came, into primary prominence. It was commonly said at the time that the prominence given to the bureaucratic group represented a reaction from the military domination; but this is hard to believe in view of the fact that Hirota was able to form a Cabinet only by securing army approval for each of his Ministers. More probably the army decided to work through the bureaucrats because it realized that it could not thrust itself forward after the February incident; it was determined that party government should be blocked and it had been disappointed in the too-liberal attitude of the two Navy Premiers. At the same time, conservative pressure finally forced Baron Ikki to resign from the presidency of the Privy Council. The reactionary Baron Hiranuma took his place.

In the Cabinet itself, while the army seemed to dictate what was to be done, Minister of War General Count Terauchi was a member of the old Choshu clique, and his connections tended more toward the

[8] It is frequently said that General Araki is the idol of the younger officers, but it seems more probable that he is their tool. His undoubtedly sincere anticapitalism led him to favor many of the reforms they demanded; but he has several times aligned himself with the group that favors abstention by military men from actual politics, preferring to leave that to reservists. This has reduced his prestige with the younger officers, but not, perhaps, his usefulness.

court circles and the financial interests than toward
the young officers. For the moment at least, the moderates had regained control in military councils;
there was reason to hope that if the military moderates and the civilian bureaucrats could manage to
work together, extremism might be avoided in both
organizations.

New factors entered the situation, however. The
"moderate-extremist" split that had already cut
across the army, the bureaucracy, and the parties,
now reached the capitalists. Mitsubishi and Sumitomo, the established firms, were clearly with the
moderates. Mitsui was uncertain; its background led
it to moderation, but many of its newer interests
directed it toward the extremists. The established
capitalists, then, were closest to the moderate bureaucrats of Hirota's type, and to the moderates in
the army. The close connection of Mitsubishi with
the navy, and the activities of navy leaders throughout the period, indicates a probable close association
of the larger part of the navy with the bureaucracy
and the "moderate" capitalist interests.

The conquest and development of Manchuria,
however, gave rise to another group of more adven-
turous and speculative capitalists who found their
most profitable association with the group of young
officers in the army. Armament and aircraft manu-
facturers, and cotton-hungry spinning firms, as well
as most interests which favored an inflationary financial policy, created a new conflict in Japan when
they supported the extremist army movement. As
a result, the extremist army element, which was the
greatest threat to parliamentary government, no
longer found itself opposed to a united capitalist
class. A new and aggressive element of that class

now vigorously backed their foreign adventures, and supported their domestic demands. Thus the conflict between the army and the bureaucrats found capitalist reinforcements on each side, all of the elements in turn being cross-riven by internal conflicts.

JAPAN ENTERS A "SEMIWAR STAGE" OF ECONOMY

The Emperor opened the sixty-ninth session of the Diet in May 1936. With a reference to the disturbance of the previous February, he commanded his subjects henceforth to suppress disharmony and work together "to advance the national destiny." Hirota's Cabinet took one path toward that goal. The Diet passed forty-five of the Government's forty-six bills, most of which indicated a definite trend toward bureaucratic totalitarianism, if not fascism. Arms figures reached a new record; diet regulations which would ruin parties were proposed; seditious literature and dangerous thought legislation was strengthened; an "Intelligence Commission," at once an information co-ordinating office and a propaganda department, was created. Taxes were increased; the nationalization of the electric power industry was begun; and import and exchange regulations were tightened. Finance Minister Baba went so far as to announce that the new budget, of which forty-six per cent went to the armed forces, would necessitate a semiwartime economic organization for the next few years, controlled by an economic "general staff."

Finally, Japan concluded a pact with Germany against communism. It was widely opposed in the country, and the Privy Council attacked Hirota vigorously for it, but it was ratified. Not long after a similar pact was made with Italy.

Not only the increasing growth of fascist or direct action societies, but the Government's activities, therefore, frightened the Diet. In the fall of 1936 an army report stated that totalitarian government was the only thing for Japan. Then rumors spread that the army favored limitation of the suffrage to heads of families and ex-service men, and demanded that no member of the Diet could hold a Government post; at this there was an uproar. The War Minister maintained that such statements did not come from him, and that no one else was qualified to speak for the army. Rumors arose again over the question of discipline in the army. There was very little direct challenge to parliamentary government; this had been given by the Meiji Emperor, and thus was not subject to criticism. The extremists clamored only for the abolition of the parties, although when War Minister Terauchi spoke to this effect to the Cabinet, and assured them that the army believed in "proper representation of the people of Japan," much indignation was reported in the army at this "exaggeration version" of the Minister's words.

In December 1936 Foreign Minister Arita resigned because of the reaction against the German-Japanese Treaty; the difficulties in the Russo-Japanese Fisheries negotiations; the independence of the Army's action in regard to "Manchoukuo's invasion" of Suiyuan; and the impossibility of settling the differences between the Home Government and the Kwantung Army, which at the moment was discovering unsurmountable differences within itself. The Cabinet managed to survive with difficulty. In January 1937, however, War Minister Terauchi came out of a bitter debate with the House of Representatives with a claim that the Army had been insulted and a demand that the House be dissolved in punishment. The four party members of the Cabinet and Navy Minister Nagano Osumi held out against dissolution, however, and instead Hirota's Cabinet resigned.

THE ARMY DEFIES THE "MODERATES," 1937

General Ugaki Kazushige was commanded to form a Cabinet. The Army refused, however, to appoint a War Minister, for Ugaki was of the moderate wing, and had long been friendly to the political parties. Recommended by the *Genro*, holding the support of press, business, and of the political parties, with the rest of his Cabinet appointed, Ugaki had nevertheless to confess his failure to the Throne. Enraged, he surrendered his commission, although he was already on the retired list. The Army, however, refused to be moved by his bitterness.

On February 2, 1937 former War Minister General Hayashi became Premier. He was of the moderate wing, and had been retired at the time of the February Incident of 1936; but he was influential among the army leaders in power since that time. The thirteen portfolios in the cabinet were distributed for the time being among eight Ministers, Hayashi himself heading the Foreign Ministry. The Navy, which had been quietly standing by its direct loyalty to the Emperor during the troubles of the past years, was represented by its own choice, Commander-in-Chief of the Grand Fleet, Yonai Mitsumasa. By the stand he had taken in the destruction of the Hirota Ministry, War Minister Terauchi had been forced to a direct repudiation of party participation in Governments; and now in the Hayashi Cabinet, for the first time no party members appeared.

Hayashi's Government, by playing one faction against another, was successful for some time. At the demand of the Diet, Terauchi left the War Ministry; but to satisfy the Army he was made Inspector General of Military Education. At the demand of liberal capitalists, Finance Minister Baba was relieved of planning further economy, and to satisfy the Navy, Yuki Toyotaro was put in his place. Even the fascists were satisfied by the appointment of Kawarada Kakichi as Home Minister. Inevitably, however, the Army felt betrayed by the favors shown the capitalists; the parties were generally enraged; and the moderate capitalists were worried by the emphasis given to armaments, and heavy industry expansion among their extremist rivals.

The un-co-operative attitude of the Diet produced an early reaction. On March 31, 1937 Premier Hayashi announced to the Lower House that it had failed to demonstrate a proper sense of seriousness, and that the Emperor had decreed its dissolution. No particular party received his favor, and despite rumors that a new party was to be formed, Premier Hayashi made no such attempt. Instructions were issued to prefectural governors and police chiefs, however, that no candidate should be permitted to speak in a manner calculated to estrange the people from the army.

Only sixty per cent of the electorate bothered to vote; yet Premier Hayashi avoided a concession of severe defeat only by announcing that he could not be defeated since he had made no effort to win the election. The *Minseito* captured 179 seats, the *Seiyukai* 175, the *Shakai Taishuto* (Social Mass

Party) made a distinct advance with 37 seats, and the remaining 75 were distributed among other groups. Despite his refusal to admit defeat, Premier Hayashi encountered difficulties. Minister of the Interior Kawarada had announced on the day before the election that they were planning a corporate state; and in May following the elections, the Privy Council called Hayashi before it to discover whom Kawarada had meant by "they" and what position Hayashi took in reference to this, and with respect to the not very much improved outlook for the new Diet's attitude toward him. By this time every faction had forgotten Hayashi's favors to itself in its resentment at his favors to the others, and no one was particularly disappointed when after concerted attacks by the parties and the House of Peers, his Cabinet fell on June 1, 1937.

PRINCE KONOE FORMS AN ALL-FACTION CABINET, 1937

On the same day the new Cabinet took office. Its Premier, Prince Konoe Fumimaro, had long been mentioned as a probable appointee to the office; he had been a protégé of Prince Saionji, and as the venerable *Genro* nominated other men during the successive crises after the Manchurian Incident of 1931, it was expected that he was holding Konoe back as his last card. A member of one of the oldest and most aristocratic families in Japan, the new Premier had succeeded Prince Tokugawa to the presidency to the House of Peers in 1933; and while in that position, had taken occasion to assert his belief that the House of Peers should have authority equal to that of the Lower House, and that the day of the two-party system was dead.

Assuming the premiership, Prince Konoe announced that he would endeavor to harmonize the differences in the nation, and would appoint to his Cabinet men of good faith and ability, regardless of whether they were "party politicians or officials." In the end, his Government was composed of one count, one airplane manufacturer, one army officer, one navy officer, and eight civilians, of whom five came from the House of Peers and three from the parties in the Lower House. As Minister of Foreign Affairs and Head of the new Cabinet Planning Board, Prince Konoe retained the experienced Hirota Koki.

A special two-week session of the Diet was called for July 23. Meanwhile, a gesture toward the parties was made in the appointment of twenty-four parliamentary Vice-Ministers and Councillors to the Cabinet. For the first time, all of them were drawn from the Lower House, according to the strength of the parties.

On July 7, however, military developments in China again had a determining effect on Japanese Government, and the possibilities of normal governmental operation under the first *Kuge* (Court Noble) Premier since Saionji's last Government in 1912, were never explored. The party politicians had definitely failed when it came to a test of strength; the militarists had strength but were unable to command any unified support, even from their own ranks, for any length of time. The bureaucrats had been unable to withstand alone the crosscurrents of the militarist-party battle. Now, with Imperial Princes at the heads of both army and navy General Staffs, with civilians in the positions closest to the

Emperor,[9] with the moderate element evidently dominant in the army despite Hayashi's fall, the appointment of a Court Noble might have provided an opportunity for a more normal sort of government better suited to Japanese conditions to develop. Almost immediately upon Konoe's appointment, however, external forces brought abnormal conditions, in which the civilian government, if it were to survive at all, had to turn more and more completely to the militarists for support.

THE CABINET RETAINS CONTROL OF FOREIGN RELATIONS

The Cabinet at once made[10] an extremely vigorous attempt to involve nonmilitary elements in the Japanese military plans, before the military could take matters over completely. On July 13, soon after the Army Command had begun to hold conferences, the Cabinet called the prefectural governors, leading industrialists, and financiers to Tokyo for consultation. The Bank of Japan was ordered to increase its gold supply, and measures were taken to keep the *yen* from falling on the foreign exchange. Before the army could move, the Cabinet threatened Nanking with stern military measures. This was not simply an attempt to keep one jump ahead of the army. The Cabinet was not extremist, but it saw that the affair was serious; that it would certainly involve the army if it were permitted to drag; and that if the Chinese realized that Japan was united, they might make military action unnecessary. If nothing

[9] Imperial Household Minister Matsudaira Tsuneo, a diplomat and son of a feudal lord (*daimyo*) to the Tokugawa; and Lord Keeper of the Privy Seal Yuasa Kurahei, of *samurai* stock.

[10] And, to the date of going to press, is still making.

else could be done, at least the army would act as an organ of the Government, not in defiance of it.

On July 15 the War Minister admitted that the first Japanese reinforcements were already en route to North China. The "Incident" of 1937, 1938, and the indeterminate future had begun. On July 23 the special two-week Diet session began, and Foreign Minister Hirota told the House that the Cabinet was prepared to take all appropriate steps in coping with what might at any moment become a dangerous situation. By August 2 the adoption of emergency taxation and commercial control measures had already put Japan on a nearly wartime basis; and two days later a supplementary budget was approved for North China use, amounting to over four hundred million *yen*, of which about one-fourth went to the Navy. On August 7 the special session ended, in an atmosphere of unity unknown for years.

As the situation continued to grow more serious, further measures were taken, and Japan marched further along the road to a wartime administration and economy. With great acumen, however, Premier Prince Konoe managed always to keep the civilian Government ahead of the Army. If Japan was to be organized on a fighting basis, it would not become an appendage to the army; it would enable itself to make most efficient use of its army.

In September 1937 Premier Konoe presented to the newly convened Diet a program for organizing Japan along the lines of a totalitarian state. The Government admitted that the conflict with China was expected to extend beyond the current year, and that it would be useless to plan short-term budgets. On September 17 a group of bankers praised the Government's stand and assured it of their support. As more and more regulatory laws went into effect, on October 14, a Cabinet Advisory Board was created. It included ten members, of whom four were from the army and navy, three from the political parties, two from finance and business, and one was a diplomat. The militarists had the largest single representation, it was true, but they would have to secure the agreement of at least two members from the other groups in order to make their views prevail.

Meanwhile, a movement in favor of formal declaration of war on China had begun to develop. The navy was reported to favor it—for by a declaration of war the delicacy of their rather anomalous blockade would have been relieved; but the army was not very enthusiastic.

On November 21, 1937 the budget for 1938 was announced. Estimated on a full wartime basis, it totaled some five billion *yen*. The appropriations for civil items alone was expected to equal the entire 1937 budget of nearly three billion *yen*, and the rest was destined for the armed services.

JAPAN IN THE "FASCIST BLOC"

Foreign indignation at the Japanese activities in China made it inevitable that the Government should lean more than ever in the direction of the fascist states of Europe. In the late fall of 1937 Italy was admitted to the German-Japanese "Anti-Comintern" Pact, and shortly afterward she recognized Manchoukuo. In December, Japan recognized the Franco regime in Spain. All sorts of bargains with Germany were rumored. No less seriously than the Western peoples who were coming to think of Germany, Italy, and Japan together as the "fascist, aggressor" nations, large sections of the Japanese people began to think that only in the Germans and the Italians could they find understanding friends.

On December 13, 1937 a Japanese army entered Nanking. Evidently given a free rein, the troops ran wild; and for the first time a breakdown of discipline, long rumored among the younger officers, was threatened among the ordinary soldiers. Measures were at once taken throughout the military and civilian organizations to weed out disunity. Labor groups at home were dissolved and 370 leaders jailed, charged with spreading antiwar propaganda and disturbing the peace. Broad shifts were made in the Army and Navy Command.

On January 10, 1938 an Imperial Council met in Tokyo. It was anticipated that it would, as had three of its four predecessors, result in a declaration of war against China. When nothing but another declaration of policy was forthcoming, rumors spread that the Emperor had pitted his determination against the Generals, and won. At the establishment of an Imperial Headquarters in the late fall of 1937, in order to centralize and concentrate direction of the war, there had been talk of eliminating the civilian cabinet, or of emasculating its authority; but Konoe's careful policy had preserved at least the form of parliamentarianism. Now, again, the asserted intention of the militarists to assume complete control and management of the state had been frustrated. Announcement was made, instead, that there was complete agreement between the Cabinet and the military and naval authorities.

TOTALITARIAN JAPAN, 1938

A weaker note was heard when, after exhortations by the War Minister to be firm in the face of possible difficulties with an unnamed third power, the Diet indicated uneasiness at the Government's failure to enlighten the people upon its aims. The National Mobilization Bill, virtually completing the totalitarian and wartime organization of the nation, was put before the Diet in February. It met with bitter opposition, although Premier Konoe promised that it would not be invoked during the "current incident." Under threat of dissolution it was finally passed—and then unanimously—on March 16. Arrests of "radicals," brutal attacks on mass party and other proletarian leaders, and growing development of reactionary and direct action groups, combined with diplomatic alignment with the fascist powers of Europe, and totalitarian organization of the domestic administration and economy, offered a demonstration, unpleasant to many but nonetheless convincing, that Japan, no matter whether she were to end in a Japanese or un-Japanese form of organization, had left the forms of liberal parliamentarianism completely.

On May 5, 1938 despite Prince Konoe's earlier statement to the Diet, the Government invoked certain provisions of the new National Mobilization Law in order to secure control of essential commodities and industries. Early in June, Cabinet changes brought General Araki Sadao—agrarian and young officer's group—to the Ministry of Education; General Ugaki Kazushige—moderate militarist favorable to parties and resentful toward the army after it blocked his proposed Cabinet in 1936—to the Foreign Ministry; and Ikeda Seihin—financier, former head of Mitsui interests until opposition of the young officers forced him to resign—to the Finance Ministry. These are strangely conflicting elements; yet with them, the Cabinet is remarkably complete. As Japan finds a real war on her hands, most of the outstanding men and most of the outstanding conflicts in her recent history are represented in her Government.

CONCLUSION

In 1889, in a Japan newly opened to strong influences from the West, a Constitution based on Western models was promulgated. The first statement in the Constitution provided that, while the vehicles of administration might conform to the new Western models, they must forever run along the path of the Imperial Way.

During the period from that year until about 1918, when the oligarchy of Elder Statesmen were in power, the elements of this new Japanese Government crystallized. The nature of this crystallization, in view of the social and economic problems facing the nation, made it inevitable that its component elements would suffer incessant friction among themselves.

At first these conflicts seemed largely restricted to personalities. It did not seem so much a conflict between civilian and military authority, as a conflict between Ito and Yamagata, or between Yamagata and Katsura. The idea of political parties early came into currency, and many of these personalities, such as Ito and Katsura, aligned themselves with parties, or formed new ones of their own, in order to gain popular support in trade for bargains with a few popular political leaders.

As the early giants of the oligarchy disappeared from the scene with the passage of time, a new class appeared—a class of professional politicians, who desired to control the government by party strength, rather than to gain popular support for an already established control of the government. The Japanese Cabinet underwent the logical development, from the German Chancellor system whereby the Premier makes a deal for support with the strongest Diet party, to the English Parliamentary system whereby the head or choice of the strongest Diet party at the moment becomes the Premier so long as his party remains strongest.

This was taken to be a healthy sign. It was not generally suspected that a basic conflict remained, not merely among the parties, but between the old oligarchical, autocratic principle on the one hand, and the whole concept of popular party government on the other. Even the military leaders seemed willing to give the party politicians a trial, and they lined up principally behind the *Seiyukai* to gain their demands. It seemed on the surface that *Kensei no Jodo*, the period of "normal," parliamentary government, was the natural successor to the earlier post-restoration period.

The peculiar circumstances surrounding the "rise to power" of the politicians, however, made it inevitable that this power could continue only at the sufferance of the military leaders. Parliamentarianism in Japan did not represent any mass movement in favor of democracy. It represented the outcome of the program of certain members of the old oligarchy, who had believed that Japan could best follow the Imperial Way in the company of the Western nations, if she was possessed of a governmental apparatus which at least superficially resembled the governmental apparatus of Germany, or of England, or of France. Now this parliamentarianism was giving rise to a new class of professional politicians, who were, in their desire to per-

petuate their power, heading toward paths which
the military class increasingly felt could only result
in disaster to Japan. These paths were not the Imperial Way. When the militarists became sufficiently
aroused on this matter to take strong action upon
it, they were able to demonstrate that their remark-
able position in the Western-model Japanese state,
dictated by the Imperial Way, gave them the power
to dispose of civil-government policy without any
necessity of a large uprising or revolution in the
Empire.

Observation of the trend of events since the military group took this action in 1931 and 1932, however, reveals certain inconsistencies. The militarists
are, supposedly, "in power." But there are still political parties in Japan. Among these parties, not
the army-supported *Seiyukai*, but the supposedly
more liberal *Minseito* has won the greatest victories
in recent election campaigns. General Ugaki was
prevented from forming a Cabinet in 1936 by the
army because he was too friendly to the political
parties; in 1938 he is Foreign Minister and supposedly the most important figure in the Cabinet.
In 1932, Ikeda Seihin was marked for destruction in
an uprising of army officers, and while he escaped
assassination, he was forced to retire from the Man-
aging Directorship of the Mitsui interests. In 1938,
he is a prominent member of the Konoe Cabinet.

The term "militarists" itself is an inconsistency.
High-ranking "militarists" have been assassinated
in army uprisings with no less enthusiasm than accompanied the murder of civilians. The elderly, diplomatic Admiral Okada is called a "militarist"; so
is "that loud trombone of destiny," General Araki.

To say, then, that the militarists are in the saddle,

and that the conflict in Japan today is clearly between the "militarists" and the nonmilitarists, is
certainly to oversimplify, if not to be downright
wrong. What ended the period of party government
in Japan was not simply the attacks of the militarists. These could not have had so ruinous an effect
were it not for the decline of the influence of the
politicians as a result of their inability to agree
on programs to settle Japanese problems in a Japanese way. Now, the period of the "militarist domination" is demonstrating that, while the nominal
leaders of the government come from the army, or
have the approval of the army high command, the
"militarists" themselves can find even less basis for
ideological solidarity than the politicians could find.

These inconsistencies are symptoms of the real
conflicts inside Japan. It is impossible to view the
"struggle for power" as a well-defined battle among
consolidated groups. The impressive part of the picture is the inability of any single group to become
consolidated. There is no clearly delineated struggle
of army against capitalists, of workers against bourgeoisie, or of agrarians against industrialists. On
some questions part of the army and part of the
capitalists are opposed to the other part of the army
and the other part of the capitalists. On most questions the alignment is far more complex. There is
not even a consistent struggle of army and bureaucracy officials against radical and liberal politicians and civilians. Each "group" is so shot through
with schisms that it has been impossible for any
single movement to control affairs in Japan completely according to its own program. The result
has been, as it is illustrated in the Konoe Cabinet,

what the West would call compromise and what Japan would call a sort of unity.

No inconsistency may seem greater than that between the bases of Japanese thought, as they were described in the first part of this book, and the present condition of the Japanese government, as it has just been depicted. In this inconsistency lies the fundamental problem of Japanese life today. What was explained in the first chapter, here, is theory rather than fact. Yet, in the face of facts which seem to belie it, it is necessary to understand that theory. It is necessary to realize that certain things which in the West are customarily considered individually, cannot be disassociated from each other in the Japanese mind. It is necessary to understand and realize all this not because it is Japanese life today, but because it is part of the traditional ideology which conditions the way in which the Japanese people face their life today. A knowledge of Japanese history is a knowledge of material disunity and bloody strife. Yet a knowledge of Japanese thought is a knowledge of an indivisible whole whose facets, directed toward the different spheres of human life and culture, must be considered together to have meaning.

New forces have entered Japanese life, and new ways of thinking are available to influence the answers which new problems are demanding. Yet this traditional ideology exercises an unabated influence upon the answers that are forthcoming. It is not yet possible to know how deeply Western economic, political, and moral ideas have penetrated into the governed masses of Japan; out of the distress which the current undertaking in China is producing will probably come the first real indication. There can be no doubt, however, that the governing classes, with the apparent support of the people, have come more and more to emphasize the Imperial Way. They claim no interest in the principles of fascism or of communism, when they are justifying their development of Japan into a totalitarian state; they turn only to the principles that should be followed by the nation whose Emperor is a god, and whose government rests on men, not laws; whose politics must be synonymous with ethics, and whose individual subjects exist only for the good of their whole community.

The greatest question, however, lies still unanswered: How, and by what instruments, may the Imperial Way best be followed? From this very malleable nature of the *Kodo* principle, from self-interests that cross all programs of class or occupational alignments, and from half-developed progeny of occidental philosophies of liberalism, fascism, and communism, come the ill-assorted conflicts that now plague Japan. So long as the various advocates of the Imperial Way are as vague as they are now in describing what their programs for *Kodo* really are, factions will continue to be torn by internal dissension. Only when all Japan knows definitely the direction in which the Imperial Way will lead and who the guides upon it will be, can the conflicts crystallize. Only then can those who oppose movement in that direction, and its guides, consistently oppose and attack consistent opponents.

When that time comes, when the large issue clearly appears, Japan may destroy herself as a great power; the attempt to resolve ancient Japanese tradition and modern occidental industrialism may end in disaster. Or it may end in success, and as she moves forward upon a concrete Imperial Way Japan may gain the greater power by finding in her own traditions an answer to a Western problem which the Western peoples have been unable to answer. Until that time comes—if it ever does come—Japan will continue in a compromise that is unceasing conflict, because no single issue is large enough to attract a majority of the factions consistently to its support.

CHARTS

The Emperor's Position in the Japanese State
The Constitution and the Imperial House Law
The Direction of the Japanese Government

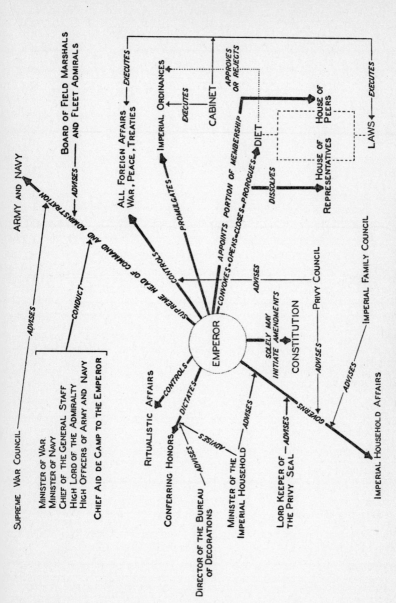

THE EMPEROR'S POSITION IN THE JAPANESE STATE

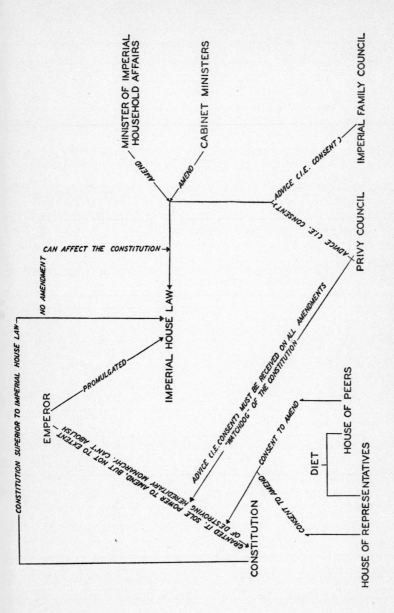

THE CONSTITUTION AND THE IMPERIAL HOUSE LAW

MINISTER OF IMPERIAL HOUSEHOLD AFFAIRS

CABINET MINISTERS

IMPERIAL FAMILY COUNCIL

PRIVY COUNCIL

—AMEND—

AMEND

ADVICE (I.E. CONSENT)

ADVICE (I.E. CONSENT)

CAN AFFECT THE CONSTITUTION →

NO AMENDMENT

IMPERIAL HOUSE LAW

CONSTITUTION SUPERIOR TO IMPERIAL HOUSE LAW

EMPEROR

—PROMULGATED—

GRANTED IT: SOLE POWER TO AMEND, BUT NOT TO EXTENT OF DESTROYING HEREDITARY MONARCHY; CAN'T ABOLISH

ADVICE (I.E. CONSENT) MUST BE RECEIVED ON ALL AMENDMENTS

"WATCHDOG" OF THE CONSTITUTION

CONSENT TO AMEND

CONSTITUTION

CONSENT TO AMEND

HOUSE OF PEERS

DIET

HOUSE OF REPRESENTATIVES

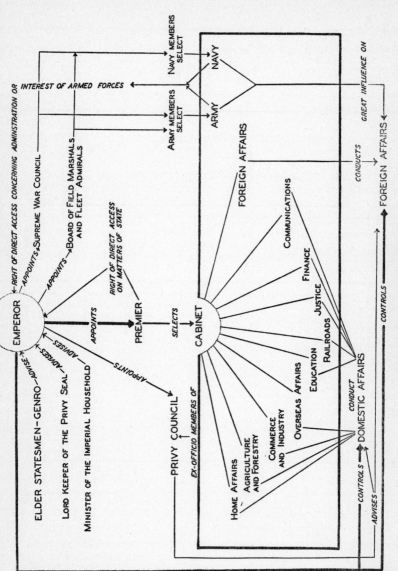

The Direction of Japanese Government

BIBLIOGRAPHY

BIBLIOGRAPHY
OF SELECTED READINGS

As THIS text is primarily intended for those beginning the study of Japanese Government, it does
not seem desirable to append to it an exhaustive
bibliography of detailed studies. Japanese sources
and western monographs formed the principal basis
for the present description of Japanese Government
and Politics; it is hoped that now there will be no
further need for students in elementary courses to
consult them, with the large and not always fruitful
expenditure of time which that involves. The present list has been compiled with an eye to further
readings in background material, and in some specific
topics discussed in this text, in a form most easily
available to the students with average library facili-
ties at their disposal. Not all of the works listed are
completely reliable, and probably many persons will
think of titles which should have been included.
There are to be found here, however, most of the
useful books in this field which are to be found in
most college libraries. Titles which students undertaking the study of Japanese institutions for the
first time are especially advised to consult are
marked by an asterisk *.

I. Sources for Background Material on Japan
   A. Historical
       Brinkley, F. and Kikuchi, D. *A History of
         the Japanese People.* New York, 1915.
       Clement, E. W. *A Short History of Japan.*
       Revised edition, Tokyo, 1926.

Hara, K. *An Introduction to the History of Japan.* New York, 1920.

Latourette, K. S. *The Development of Japan.* New York, 1918.

Murdoch, J. *A History of Japan.* (3 Vols.) London, 1926.

*Sansom, G. B. *Japan, A Short Cultural History.* London, 1935.

Steiger, G. N. *History of the Far East.* Boston, 1936.

Treat, P. T. *The Far East.* Revised edition, New York, 1935.

B. Economic

Bain, H. F. *Ores and Industry in the Far East.* New York, 1933.

Hindmarsh, A. *Bases of Japanese Foreign Policy.* Cambridge, 1936.

*Honjo, E. *Economic and Social History of Japan.* Kyoto, 1935.

Ishii, R. *Population Pressure and Economic Life in Japan.* London, 1937.

Moulton, H. G. *Japan: An Economic and Financial Appraisal.* Washington, 1931.

*Orchard, J. and D. *Japan's Economic Position.* New York, 1930.

Takekoshi, Y. *Economic Aspects of the History of the Civilization of Japan.* (3 Vols.) London, 1930.

C. Reference Works

Chamberlain, B. H. *Things Japanese.* Revised edition, London, 1927.

Nachod, O. *Bibliography of the Japanese Empire.* 1928 (2 Vols.), 1931, 1935, 1937. This continues von Wenckstern, below;

the 1937 volume, the fifth in the series,
reaches 1935.

Papinot, E. *Dictionary of the History and
Geography of Japan.* Yokohama, 1910.

Trewartha, G. T. *A Reconaissance Geography of Japan.* Madison, Wis., 1934.

von Wenckstern, Fr. *Bibliography of the
Japanese Empire.* (2 Vols.) 1895, 1907.
Covers period 1859-1906.

II. JAPANESE POLITICAL THOUGHT

Abe Iso. "Socialism in Japan." In *Fifty Years
of New Japan,* edited by Okuma, S. London,
1909. (Vol. II, pp. 494-512.)

Anesaki, M. *History of Japanese Religion.* London, 1930.

Armstrong, R. C. *Light from the East: Studies
in Japanese Confucianism.* Toronto, 1913.

Aston, W. G. *Shinto, the Way of the Gods.*
London, 1905.

Colegrove, K. W. *Militarism in Japan.* ("World
Affairs Books" No. 16) Boston, 1936.

Eliot, C. *Japanese Buddhism.* London, 1935.

Fujisawa, C. *Japanese and Oriental Political
Philosophy.* Tokyo, 1935.

*Fukuzawa Yukichi *Autobiography.* (Translated
by Kiyooka, E.) Tokyo, 1935. The charm-
ingly written autobiography of an outstanding liberal, the founder of Keio University.

Holtom, D. C. *The Japanese Enthronement
Ceremonies.* Tokyo, 1928.

——— *The Political Philosophy of Modern
Shinto.* Vol. XLIX, Pt. II of the *Transactions of the Asiatic Society of Japan.* Tokyo,
1922.

Hozumi, N. *Ancestor Worship and Japanese Law.* Revised edition, Tokyo, 1912.

Ito Hirobumi. *Commentaries on the Constitution of the Empire of Japan.* (Translated by Ito Miyoji.) 2nd edition, Tokyo, 1906.

Kato, G. *A Study of Shinto, the Religion of the Japanese Nation.* Tokyo, 1926.

Nitobe, I. *Bushido, the Soul of Japan.* New York, 1905.

—— *Japanese Traits and Foreign Influences.* London, 1927.

—— (ed.) *Western Influences in Modern Japan.* Chicago, 1931.

Ozaki, Y. *The Voice of Japanese Democracy.* Yokohama, 1918.

Reischauer, A. K. *Studies in Japanese Buddhism.* New York, 1916.

Suzuki, D. T. *Zen Buddhism and Its Influence on Japanese Culture.* Kyoto, 1938.

Tanin, O. and Yohan, E. *Militarism and Fascism in Japan.* New York, 1934.

III. The Evolution of the Japanese Government Until 1889

Asakawa, K. *The Early Institutional Life of Japan.* Tokyo, 1903.

Brinkley, F. and Kikuchi, D. *A History of the Japanese People.* New York, 1915.

Gubbins, J. H. *The Progress of Japan.* Oxford, 1911. Covers period 1853-1871.

Hara, K. *An Introduction to the History of Japan.* New York, 1920.

McLaren, W. W. *Japanese Government Documents.* Vol. XLII, Pt. I of the *Transactions of the Asiatic Society of Japan,* Tokyo, 1914.

Includes most of the important documents for the period of 1868-1889.

Murdoch, J. *A History of Japan.* (3 Vols.) London, 1926.

Nachod, O. *Geschichte von Japon.* (3 Vols.) Gotha, 1906. From beginnings to 850 A.D.

Reischauer, R. K. Early Japanese History. ca. 40 B.C.-A.D. 1167. (2 Vols.) Princeton, 1937.

*Sansom, G. B. *Japan, A Short Cultural History.* London, 1935.

Uehara, G. E. *Political Development of Japan 1867-1909.* New York, 1910.

Wedemeyer, A. *Japänische Frühgeschichte.* Tokyo, 1930.

IV. THE ESTABLISHMENT OF CONSTITUTIONAL GOVERNMENT

Ito Hirobumi. *Commentaries on the Constitution of the Empire of Japan.* (Translated by Ito Miyoji) 2nd edition, Tokyo, 1906.

McLaren, W. W. *Japanese Government Documents.* Vol. XLII. Pt. I of the *Transactions of the Asiatic Society of Japan.* Tokyo, 1914.

*——— A Political History of Japan During the Meiji Era. London, 1916.

Matsunami, N. *The Constitution of Japan.* Tokyo, 1930.

Uehara, G. E. *Political Development of Japan 1867-1909.* New York, 1910.

V. THE PRESENT ORGANIZATION OF THE JAPANESE GOVERNMENT

Colegrove, K. W. "The Japanese Cabinet." *American Political Science Review.* Vol. XXX, No. 5, 1936.

———— "The Japanese Emperor." *American Political Science Review*. Vol. XXVI, Nos. 4 and 5, 1932.

———— "The Japanese Foreign Office." *American Journal of International Law*. Vol. XXX, No. 4, 1936.

———— "The Japanese Privy Council." *American Political Science Review*. Vol. XXV, Nos. 3 and 4, 1931.

———— *Militarism in Japan*. ("World Affairs Books" No. 16) Boston, 1936.

———— "Powers and Function of the Japanese Diet." *American Political Science Review*. Vol. XXVII, No. 6, 1933, and Vol. XXVIII, No. 1, 1934.

Ito Hirobumi. *Commentaries on the Constitution of the Empire of Japan*. (Translated by Ito Miyoji) 2nd edition, Tokyo, 1906.

Kitazawa, N. *The Government of Japan*. Princeton, 1929.

Labatt-Simon, H. M. G. "The Japanese Military Machine." *Amerasia*, Vol. I, No. 12, 1938.

Matsunami, N. *The Constitution of Japan*. Tokyo, 1930.

Nakano, T. *Ordinance Power of the Japanese Emperor*. Baltimore, 1923.

Okuma, E. Ed. *Fifty Years of New Japan*. (2 Vols.) London, 1909. Articles by Ito on the Constitution, Itagaki, Ukita, and Okuma on political parties, and Abe on socialism.

Quigley, H. S. *Japanese Government and Politics*. New York, 1932.

Takeuchi, T. *War and Diplomacy in the Japanese Empire*. New York, 1935. Describes the structure of the government in order to explain the control of foreign policy.

VI. THE EVOLUTION OF JAPANESE GOVERNMENT SINCE 1889

Bisson, T. A. *Japan in China*. New York, 1938.

——— "The Trend Toward Dictatorship in Japan." *Foreign Policy Report*. February 13, 1935.

Colegrove, K. W. "Labor Parties in Japan." *American Political Science Review*. Vol. XXIII, No. 2, 1929.

——— *Militarism in Japan*. ("World Affairs Books" No. 16), Boston, 1936.

Fujisawa, R. *The Recent Aims and Political Development of Japan*. New Haven, 1923.

Lederer, E. and E. *Japan in Transition*. New Haven, 1938.

*McLaren, W. W. *A Political History of Japan During the Meiji Era*. London, 1916.

Reischauer, R. K. "Conflicts Inside Japan." *Harper's Magazine*. July, 1936.

——— "The Disunity of the Japanese Militarists." *Amerasia*, Vol. I, No. 1, 1937.

——— "Japan's Road to War." *Asia Magazine*. February, 1937.

Takeuchi, T. *War and Diplomacy in the Japanese Empire*. New York, 1935.

Tanin, O. and Yohan, E. *Militarism and Fascism in Japan*. New York, 1934.

———, ——— *When Japan Goes to War*. New York, 1936. Gives useful details of the integrated structure of the modern Japanese state-nation.

Young, A. M. *Japan Under Taisho Tenno, 1912-1926*. London, 1928.

—— *Imperial Japan*. 1926-1938.

GLOSSARY

GLOSSARY

THE translations of a number of Japanese terms and an index to further explanations in the text of certain terms and titles are given below. As for pronunciation of Japanese words, the consonants are spoken as in English, the vowels as in Italian.

Amaterasu-Omikami: The Sun Goddess, 25.
Amatsu-kami: Deities of Heaven.
Ashigaru: Light troops in feudal armies, 51.

Bakufu: The bureaucracy which carried on the government under the *Shoguns*; the *Shogunate*.
Be: Hereditary organizations of farmers, artisans, etc., in the early period, 40.
Buke: Feudal barons, 49.
Bushi: Military class of warriors also known as *samurai*, 47-48.

Chiji: The title given to *daimyo* as provincial governors during the interim between the abolition of feudalism and the establishment of the Home Industry, 66.
Chonin: Townsmen class or bourgeoisie, 62.

Daijin: Minister of a ministry (i.e., of the Ministry of War, etc.) 64(note).
Daimyo: Feudal barons, 52-53.
Dai Nippon: Japan.
Dajodaijin: Prime Minister, 64(note).

Kenseito: "The Party for Constitutional Government," formed in 1898 by the fusion of the *Jiyuto* and *Shimpoto*, 117.

Kizoku-in: The House of Peers, 84-85.

Kodo: "The Imperial Way," 33, 39, 193-194.

Kokoku Seinen Shoko Domei: "The Young Officers' League," 174.

Koku: The unit of measure, one of which equals 5.11 dry American bushels.

Kokuhonsha: "A (Reactionary) Nationalist Society," 164.

Kokumin Domei: "The National Union Party" (Fascist), formed by *Adachi* in 1932, 162.

Kokuryu-kai: "The Black Dragon Society," 93 (note).

Kuge: Court nobles.

Kunaidaijin: Minister of the Imperial Household, 86.

Kuni-no-miyatsuko: Local chieftains, 42.

Kunitsu-kami: Deities of Earth.

Kyochokai: An organized reactionary pressure group formed in 1919 by representatives of both capital and labor, 138.

Meiji Restoration: 1867, the overthrow of the *Tokugawa Shogunate*, and the return of the temporal, as well as the spiritual power to the Emperor, 56-58.

Minseito: "The Party for Popular Government," the former *Kenseikai*, formed in 1928, 96, 150, 152-153(note).

Naidaijin: Lord Keeper of the Privy Seal, 72, 86.

Naikaku: The Cabinet, 100-101.

Naikaku Shigikai: Cabinet Inquiry Council, established 1935, 169.

Nakatomi: A prominent clan in the early period of Japanese history, 46.

Nirvana: The *Buddhist* Paradise.

Nomin Rodoto: The Farmer-Labor Party, founded in 1927, 146.

Norito: *Shinto* liturgies.

Nuhi: Slaves, 40.

Rikken Doshikai: "Constitutional Fellow-Thinkers' Society" founded by *Katsura* in 1913, later became the *Kenseikai*, 128-129.

Ronin: Lordless *samurai*, 55.

Roninkai: Organized reactionary pressure group formed in 1918, by "freelancers" for unaffiliated groups, 138.

Sadaijin: The Great Minister of the Left, 64(note).

Sam-bo: The Three *Buddhist* Treasures, 25.

Samurai: The military class; retainers of the feudal barons, 52-53.

Sangi: Imperial Adviser, 64(note).

Seiyu-honto: "The 'Real' (honto) Organization of Political Friends," a faction which split from the *Seiyukai* in 1921, 142.

Seiyukai: "The Political Friends' Organization" successor to the Kenseito, founded by Prince *Ito* in 1900, 96, 152-153(note).

Shakai-taishuto: "The People's Socialist Party," or "The Social Mass Party," formed in 1932 by fusion of the *Shakai Minshuto* (Social Democrats), and the *Zenkoku-Rono-Taishuto* (National Farmer-Labor Party), 97, 162.

Shimpoto: "The Progressive Party," *Okuma's* party, established 1896, 116-117.

Shinto: The national cult of Japan, 25-26, 27-28.
Sho: Ministry (e.g., of War, Communications), 64 (note).
Shoen: Feudal manor, 47.
Shogun: Military Dictator, 48-49, 52.
Shogunate: Military dictatorship and its bureaucracy, 52-56.
Shugi-in: The House of Representatives, 94-95.
Shugo: Military deputies of the *Shogun*, 48.
Soshi: Organized hired bullies, 140.
Sumitsu-in: The Privy Council, 72, 87-89.
Sutra: A holy book of Buddhism.

Taisho: "Great Righteousness," the name of the era and of the Emperor during the period 1912-1926.
T'ang: Chinese dynasty, 618-907 A.D., 44.
Teikoku-zaigo-gunjin-kai: "The Imperial Ex-Servicemen's Association," 93.
Tenno: A Japanese word meaning Emperor.
T'ien: In *Confucianism*, the concept of "The Will of Heaven," 28.
Tozama-daimyo: Feudal barons hostile to the *Tokugawa Shogunate*, 52.

Udaijin: The Great Minister of the Right, 64(note).
Uji: Clan, 40.
Uji-bito: Members of a clan, 40.
Uji-gami: A clan deity.
Uji-no-kami: Clan chieftains, 40.

Vairoçana: The Supreme *Buddha*, 25.

Za: Merchant guilds, 50.

HARBIN

MANCHUKUO

HSINKING ✛   KIRIN

MUKDEN

Yalu River

ANTUNG

KOREA

PEIPING

TIENTSIN

DAIREN
PORT ARTHUR

SEOUL

CHINA

TSINGTAO

YELLOW
SEA

Map made by Jean Reischauer